LAKE FLY-FISHING MANIFESTO

WRITTEN & ILLUSTRATED by MIKE CROFT

Frank Amato

PORTLAND

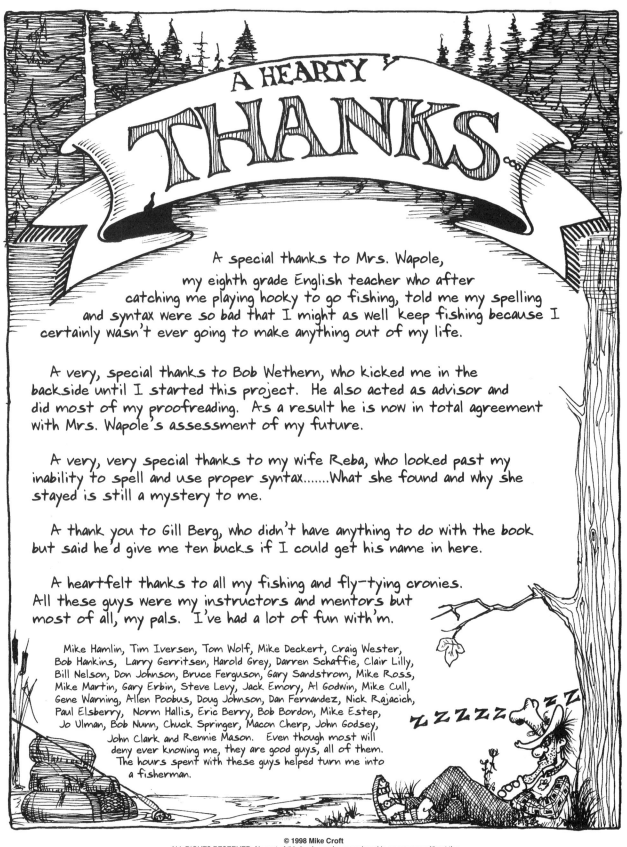

A HEARTY THANKS...

A special thanks to Mrs. Wapole,
my eighth grade English teacher who after
catching me playing hooky to go fishing, told me my spelling
and syntax were so bad that I might as well keep fishing because I
certainly wasn't ever going to make anything out of my life.

A very, special thanks to Bob Wethern, who kicked me in the backside until I started this project. He also acted as advisor and did most of my proofreading. As a result he is now in total agreement with Mrs. Wapole's assessment of my future.

A very, very special thanks to my wife Reba, who looked past my inability to spell and use proper syntax.......What she found and why she stayed is still a mystery to me.

A thank you to Gill Berg, who didn't have anything to do with the book but said he'd give me ten bucks if I could get his name in here.

A heartfelt thanks to all my fishing and fly-tying cronies. All these guys were my instructors and mentors but most of all, my pals. I've had a lot of fun with'm.

Mike Hamlin, Tim Iversen, Tom Wolf, Mike Deckert, Craig Wester, Bob Hankins, Larry Gerritsen, Harold Grey, Darren Schaffie, Clair Lilly, Bill Nelson, Don Johnson, Bruce Ferguson, Gary Sandstrom, Mike Ross, Mike Martin, Gary Erbin, Steve Levy, Jack Emory, Al Godwin, Mike Cull, Gene Warning, Allen Poobus, Doug Johnson, Dan Fernandez, Nick Rajacich, Paul Elsberry, Norm Hallis, Eric Berry, Bob Bordon, Mike Estep, Jo Ulman, Bob Nunn, Chuck Springer, Macon Cherp, John Godsey, John Clark and Rennie Mason. Even though most will deny ever knowing me, they are good guys, all of them. The hours spent with these guys helped turn me into a fisherman.

Published in 1998 by:
Frank Amato Publications, Inc.
P.O. Box 82112 • Portland, Oregon 97282 • 503-653-8108 • www.amatobooks.com

ISBN 10: 1-57188-410-6 • ISBN 13: 978-1-57188-410-7 • UPC: 0-81127-00244-3

Book Design: Mike Croft

Printed in Hong Kong

3 5 7 9 10 8 6 4 2

CONTENTS

INTRODUCTION

This is a pretty simple book to use. If you are unsure or nervous about your ability to fly fish in lake and pond environments then this book is for you. Read it through a couple of times and then get a season under your belt. After the season closes then put this book on the back of the toilet and once a day for five minutes or so compare situations you encountered with ones I write about here. In your imagination, fish all the places a second time, correcting mistakes and doing some things differently.

By the time your second season starts you will be surprisingly adept at stillwater fly fishing. You should find that you don't dislike lakes but actually look forward to fishing them. Even planning trips to them. At the end of the second season, move up to a book that will cover more of the science, the ph levels, barometric influences, etc. At this time, take this poor old book and pass it on to someone who is where you were when you got this.

Oh! One more thing...

DON'T LAUGH FIVE MINUTES A DAY IN THE ···ER··· LIBRARY WILL MAKE YOU A BETTER FISHERMAN!

FEAR OF FROG WATER

STILLWATER PSYCHOLOGICAL BARRIERS

Lake fishing requires a different mindset than river fishing. On a creek, river, or stream, an angler can cast over most, if not all, of the fish. This feature has been referred to as "intimate fishing." Lakes are a lot less "user-friendly." This is, of course, because the water is hard to read and there just isn't enough time to cover every square foot at every depth. In a stream, every fish has already seen all the flies of every angler. In the more impersonal frog water, it is likely, if not probable, that the fish have not seen a fly in a week or two. Gain confidence in this reality and convert fear into confidence.

IN A STREAM I CAN READ THE WATER, BUT NOT IN A LAKE!!

True and False! True: The stream is easier to read.
...and False! Lakes can also be read, but the angler has to take a more macro view. The position of the fish is much more in a state of flux. Other factors influence the fine art of water reading, such as the season, time of day, geography, temperature, and bug hatches.

5

Even though, in the impersonal lakes, the fish move up and down in the water column, and in and out from shore, there are some real advantages to fishing the frog water....... For example:

CASTING SKILLS ARE NOT AS IMPORTANT.

YOUR BASIC CAST WILL COVER 99% OF MOST CONDITIONS.

There are times on windy days or when fishing under brushy overhangs when you might mend or employ some fancy casting, but "up stream and dry" is not a stillwater term.

Most lakes have a captive population of fish. The trick is to find'em. Give it some thought ...after all, where are they going to go??

Fish that live in streams live on a treadmill, while fish in lakes have a more leisurely existence. Not having to expend as much energy searching for food means that they can grow bigger....

FASTER!

MT. EVEREST

There's a common superstition among fly fishermen that the more gadgets, gizmos, gimmicks, and goodies you can hang from your vest or cram in your bag, the better fisherman you will become. It is, of course, pure superstitious hogwash. I do, however, make a monthly pilgrimage to the fly shop to pick up any new stuff just in case they might be right!

NOW, LET'S TAKE A GANDER AT SOME OF THE BIG STUFF YOU JUST CAN'T LIVE WITHOUT. NOW I AIN'T GONNA COVER ALL THE CHARTS AND GRAPHS RELATING LINE WEIGHT AN' STUFF, AS YOU CAN GET ALL THAT FROM SOME OF THE BEGINNING BOOKS ON FLY FISHING.

RODS

Show 'em a little respect and call them "rods," not "poles." Poles are what you use to hold up the tent.

Rods come in many weights and lengths. Just to make things worse they also have different actions. For still waters, your rod should be between 8 1/2 to 9 1/2 feet long and, to start, should be between a 5- and an 8-weight. The heavier-weight rods are a must if the wind is a big factor where you fish. For the most part, picking out a rod is kinda personal like picking out underwear. Some like boxers, some like briefs or bikinis, and some just don't wear 'em at all. If your not sure

ask your local fly shop for their suggestions, keeping in mind that you will fish best with some-thing you're comfortable with.

Warning: Too long a rod makes landing a fish difficult.

When was the last time you saw a Spey rod in a float tube?? Action, on the other hand, is important.

Your rod has two major functions: To deliver the fly line, and to act as a shock absorber to protect the tippet. These two functions are more related to action than are rod length or weight. A fast-action rod will do better in distance casting, but worse in tippet protection. A soft or slow-action rod won't give you the distance, but will protect finer tippets.

TRUTH

Truth is an inescapable principle of our universe, kinda like death and taxes.

One of these truths is that no piece of equipment, rod, boat, fly, or what have you, is perfect. Everything we use is an accumulation of compromises. Think of a teeter-totter with all the positive stuff on one side and all the negative on the other. With a universe in balance you can't change a piece of equipment by adding a positive without moving the fulcrum or adding a negative. It is as important to know what your equipment won't do as it is to know what it will do.

CONS   PROS

Don't be seduced into picking out your stuff by looking only at the positive side. I'll try and show the shortfalls as we look at equipment. That way you won't have to make all the mistakes I already have. Give a little thought to selecting equipment, ask around, if you can, try it out. Do this and you won't make too many mistakes.

Now I know some of the rod manufacturers will scream, but your rod is not critical. Long or short, fast-action or slow, really doesn't matter as much as your choice of lines and tippets. Don't get me wrong, but the closer you get to the fish the more important stuff becomes. Ending in the fly, of course.

Simply put...A fisherman with a poor choice in rods but with the proper lines, tippets, and flies will fish circles around the fisherman who has the proper rod but the wrong lines and flies. There

are three kinds of fly lines that each are a must for the lake fisherman. Each comes in a weight-forward option. Although distance is not critical, these lines are easier to shoot and will improve distance casting. They are:

Floating: The workhorse of fly lines for daylight fishing. A must for spring and fall when fish are close to the surface.

Sink Tip: Third in importance to the lake fisherman and covers the narrow slot below the floater and above the full-sink. Stay away from the real heavy sink tips like the 300, 400, and 500 grain types. These are for steelhead, and special situations.

Full Sinking: A weight-forward with an intermediate sink rate should be your first choice. A second line with a fast sink rate is invaluable if you are fishing big water and need to get down 15 to 20 feet.

The most useful line is your floater, as it is used to...

1 ...Fish dries anywhere on the lake

2 ...Fish nymphs along the shore and among the weeds.

3 ...and to fish chironomids and nymphs below a strike indicator.

The next most useful line is a full-sinking, with an intermediate sink rate. This line is used to...

12"-36"

fish nymphs, streamers, and Woolly Buggers a foot to three feet under the surface.

HINT: THE ABOVE TWO LINES ARE SO USEFUL I KEEP THEM ON TWO IDENTICAL RODS SO I DON'T HAVE TO CHANGE LINES OFTEN ON THE WATER

There are times you need to get down deeper to find fish.

This is the time to put on a full-sinker with a fast or extra fast sink rate, and...

...work the water 10 to 25 feet deep.

NYMPH on a dry line

NYMPH on a 10' sink tip.

On occasions, trout will come to a nymph fished on a short sink-tip much better than a nymph fished just below the surface, from a floating line. It is a mystery why just an inch or two will make such a difference. Frankly, I just don't know.

Having all these different lines means changing them on occasion while you are on the water. Be aware that there is a danger of breaking your rod while changing your fly line, (especially if the fish are busting around you on the surface and you get in a hurry).

Rod companies repair hundreds of rods each year because of these two occurrences. Both can happen playing large fish, but only the "high line break" can happen while changing fly lines. Should a nail knot or braided loop hang up in a guide, then too much pressure will cause the rod to bend only at the tip. Too much bend equals one expensive repair! When the rod is held almost vertical, a large fish close to the net, making a

THE HiGH LiNE... ...BREAK

last lunge, can also produce the same result. An angler has to be ready to instantly drop the rod tip if a lunge occurs. When changing fly lines from a boat or float tube, you only need to lower the rod over the side, stringing the guides as you go making sure the ferrules are tight!

NOTE: No stress on the rod at all.

NOTE: The water won't hurt a thing, just keep the reel out of the bottom goop.

WHICH iS A LEAD iN TO THE LOOSE FERRULE BREAK.

PROPER SEATING

* IMPROPER SEATING

FORCE

FORCE

* EXAGGERATED OF COURSE

A loose ferrule puts all the pressure on two points. A big fish can cause your rod to break. Wax the male ferrule and snugly seat both the male and female ends together. This will transfer the forces from the tip section to the butt section. along a

When a rod breaks, it happens in the areas just above or below ferrules. If your rod tip keeps coming loose, it is a warning that it's time to wax the ferrule.

WAX →

HECK, I JUST USE A LITTLE BIRTHDAY CANDLE!! THEY SEEM TO BE EASIER TO FIND EVERY YEAR!

NOTE: MOST RODS THAT FAIL FROM A FLAW IN THE BLANK DO SO THE FIRST COUPLE OF TIMES THAT THEY ARE FISHED. RODS THAT FAIL AFTER THAT PERIOD ARE OFTEN THE RESULT OF SOME INCIDENT PRECIPITATED BY THE ANGLER.

It is useful to have your leader-tippet combination two feet longer than the visibility of the water. In most cases nine feet is minimum, with the longer leaders over twelve feet becoming hard to handle, (in a wind ...impossible). For convenience, nothing beats commercial tapered leaders. The 7 1/2- and 9-foot leaders are the most useful lengths. When you add a couple of feet of tippet material, the overall length fits right into our target length. Always add tippet material to the commercial tapered leaders; it saves a lot of money.

There is no need to go into tippet diameters and the "X" system, as every beginning book has them.

HEHE

The size tippet that gives you the most hook-ups with the least amount of lost fish is 5X. Use this as your starting point and work up and down in size from 5X. Ninety percent of your fishing will fall in the 4X, 5X, and 6X range. I skip sizes on either side of this central core, carrying every other size. 0X, 2X, 4X, 5X, 6X, and the smallest, 8X, rounds out my tippet selection.

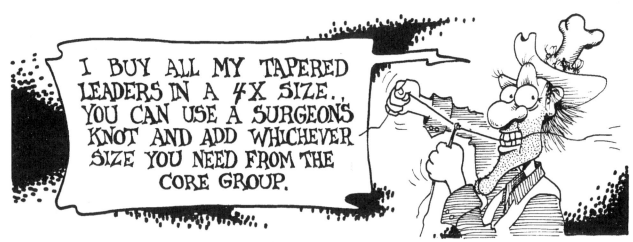

I BUY ALL MY TAPERED LEADERS IN A 4X SIZE. YOU CAN USE A SURGEONS KNOT AND ADD WHICHEVER SIZE YOU NEED FROM THE CORE GROUP.

As you keep adding tippets the original tapered leader gets shorter and larger in diameter. I save these for using with the 0X and 2X tippet materials. As for going smaller, you should tie a foot-and-a-half piece of 6X tippet on to your 4X tapered leader. To this piece you can add a couple of feet of 8X. This is a last resort tactic used in moments of desperation, when fish are being super leader shy. Remember 8X breaks real easy.

The "0X" tippet is used for night fishing and for bass, if the trout don't want to come out and play.

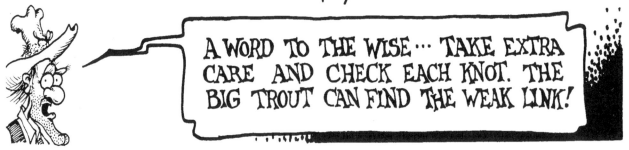

A WORD TO THE WISE ⋯ TAKE EXTRA CARE AND CHECK EACH KNOT. THE BIG TROUT CAN FIND THE WEAK LINK!

Almost as many fish are lost from bad knots as from broken tippets. Just keep reading 'cuz we will talk about this some more.

HERE ARE SOME LITTLE HINTS ABOUT NYLON LEADERS AN' TIPPETS!

Nylon can absorb about 1/3 of its weight in water. This is why a leader that has been fished subsurface needs to be dressed prior to switching back to fishing a dry fly. If the leader is not dressed it will continue to sink.

Nylon comes in hard and soft types. Hard nylon is prized for its ability to withstand abrasion and for superior knot strength. There is a desire to use this for tippet material, but if it is colored or dyed it just won't work during daylight hours. The tippet must always be clear.

Hard nylon turns over large flies better and so can make ideal leaders for night fishing and bass fishing.

Both soft and hard nylon will be glossy. This can be removed by pulling the tippet through a leader straightener.

When fishing dries, always leave the front six inches undressed so it will waterlog and sink. The imprint of only the fly will appear in the surface film.

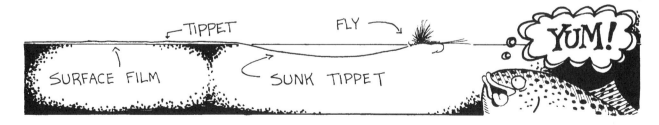

Well, we've gotta put all these lines, tippets, and leaders on something, so let's take a gander at.......

REELS: ROUND=TOOLS=FOR=FLAT=WATER

Reels fall into three categories, based on how they are manufactured: assembled, cast and,

machined. Reels that are assembled are put together with screws and major parts are stamped out of sheet metal. These are the least- expensive reels to purchase. The mid-priced and most popular reels are cast. These reels have major parts cast out of aluminum. The most expensive and most coveted reels are machined. These are cut out of bar stock aluminum which is often compressed to get the molecules packed closer together for added strength. This means if you drop it, it has less chance of warping or going out of round.

It is a constant amazement that so many anglers put so much emphasis on a drag system when we are fishing for trout. That first run happens so fast that if you have time to adjust the drag, just as often as not, in the excitement, it's

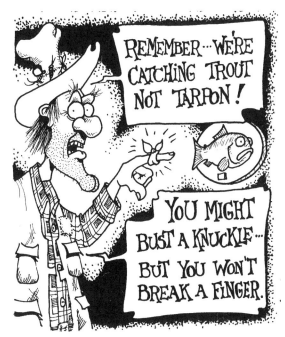

REMEMBER...WE'RE CATCHING TROUT NOT TARPON!

YOU MIGHT BUST A KNUCKLE... BUT YOU WON'T BREAK A FINGER.

turned the wrong way and.....snap! It is critical that you have a reel you can palm. Most reels come with this feature designed into the spool. Don't get me wrong, the expensive reels are a joy to use, if for no other reason, the parts and balance are so good that they function silky smooth and without wobbles, grinds and other minor nuisances. If money were no object, I would buy all my reels from this category. Money is always the lament of the trout bum. Although I have a couple of expensive reels, I own mostly reels from the second category.

Most of us have to budget our money and there is a way to help ensure our time on the water is not spoiled by a reel that won't function. I have advised you to start with three lines that will cover most situations. Most of us would buy one reel and two extra spools. Although it is the cheapest combination, if the reel is dropped and bent then all three lines are out of commission. I suggest you buy two reels and one extra spool; this way if you drop a reel you still have another that will fit all your spools. You will also be able to fish during the period that your broken reel travels back and forth from the factory. As most repairs are done high in the mountains of Tibet it can take a long time before you see your little friend again and if you have another trip planned during that period... well it is not unusual for a broken reel to screw up more than one trip.

Add up the cost of two reels and one spool as well as one reel and two spools when you have

HAA HA HA

decided on a particular make and model of reel. The difference is what your insurance costs for not being knocked out of the game.

Once in a while, a dropped reel will bend the spool. Look close at where it is scraping or pinched and sometimes you can bend it back. If you cannot bend it back, then choose the least useful line for your conditions on that day (you never bend the spool on your least useful line) and spool it off. Respool the line from your bent spool and start fishing. I've seen just as many trips ruined from a dropped reel as from a broken rod.

There are some lakes you can fish from shore, but most frog fishermen prefer to get out on the water in some sort of boat. Let's look at the options from the smallest to the largest.

THE BELLY BOAT

Originally invented by southern bass fishermen, this piece of equipment has done more to revolutionize fly fishing in lakes than any other recent development.

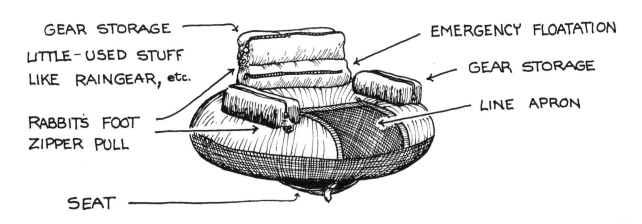

GEAR STORAGE
LITTLE-USED STUFF
LIKE RAINGEAR, etc.

RABBITS FOOT
ZIPPER PULL

SEAT

EMERGENCY FLOATATION

GEAR STORAGE

LINE APRON

As nothing is perfect, there are some disadvantages, as well as some sterling advantages, with the belly boat.

Pros.....
* Compact storage, like in a car trunk.
* Easily packed into lakes without launch ramps.
* Close to the water to better see insect activity.
* As you are suspended 3/4 in the water, they are very comfortable.
* They don't spook the fish as much as a boat does.

and Cons....
* Terrible performance in the wind.
* Slow (maximum speed is about two miles per hour).
* Difficult to launch and to move about on shore.
* Impossible to go to the bathroom while you're in one. (Not for beer drinkers.)
* Requires a hand, foot or car pump.

There is an open-ended float tube that allows for easier and safer boarding when launching. They all come with different names, depending on the manufacturer. Some are supposed to be streamlined and faster, but make no mistake....the Olympics are not planning to feature belly boat races now or in the future. What they do have is a very lightweight bladder that weighs much less than the truck tube used to inflate the standard belly boat. This is a big plus if you intend to pack-in to the high mountain lakes.

THE OPEN-ENDED BELLY BOAT...FROM ABOVE.

As you can put on your fins while you are seated in the open-ended float tube, launching is much, much easier. What you lose is the arm support from the complete wrap-around tube in the standard belly boat. This is very useful while nymph fishing. Give **considerable thought to your choice of a float tube!**

RESTING YOUR ARM GIVES EXCELLENT CONTROL OVER SLOW RETRIEVES!

Whatever type tube you settle on, look for these features:
* Quick release seat buckle for a fast exit should your tube deflate. It'll be between your legs on a standard float tube.
* Back-up floatation bladder in the backrest. It is very important and is usually an extra.
* Self-healing zippers, in case you go over the mountains and forget to let some air out of your tube. The change in pressure is guaranteed to pop your zippers. The self-healing zippers can regain their function.

"Personal water craft" always sounded a little affected to me, and also a little expensive. It seems most in this category are catamarans equipped with oars that keep your backside just above the water line. Until I used one, I thought that you would set too high and that the wind would blow you around like a Spanish galleon. However, the oars counteract that tendency and move you with more speed and ease than a traditional float tube. This will be a big advantage on medium and large lakes as it doubles or triples your fishing radius. However, fins are a must to hold you in position so you can drop the oars and pick up a rod.

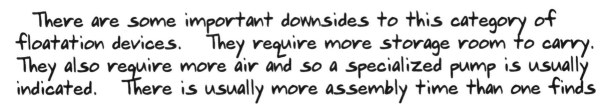

There are some important downsides to this category of floatation devices. They require more storage room to carry. They also require more air and so a specialized pump is usually indicated. There is usually more assembly time than one finds with a traditional float tube.   If you like river fishing (and who doesn't) some of the models are designed to handle up to Class 3 water, while the standard float tube is a death trap on rivers.

There are two major disadvantages to catamarans from a fishing standpoint. The first is that there is no forearm rest for fishing very slow retrieves. The second is that your head is about three feet above the level of the water and you can't see the hatches start as easily as you can in the standard float tube. You wouldn't think that a foot and a half would make much difference but it does.

Both float tubes and personal water craft require waders.   As you probably already have stream experience, I don't need to cover these in detail.   Neoprene waders are almost a standard in float tubing and come in several thicknesses.   The colder the water, the thicker your waders should be.   In real cold water you will want to wear long underwear and sweat pants or a wader liner, even then I've been in water that eventually drives me out.

You just can't avoid Latin when it comes to fly fishing. Neoprene comes from two Latin words, "Neo," which means new, and "parene," which means leak. Everyone who has owned a pair knows the definition well. One of the rites of spring is the annual wader patching day.   I consider myself the world's leading authority on wader patching.   I have lost at least a half dozen bouts with barbed wire fences. I've done hand-to-hand combat with thorny Russian olive trees and sprinted through blackberry patches evading swarms of hornets.   My waders have more patches than an African phone line.

Bar none, the best patching system is to

get an iron-on patch for the outside of the waders and a tube of silicone or latex for the inside. It might take a little longer, but you won't ever have to do them twice.   I think I have the oldest pair of functioning neoprene waders in America. No matter how old neoprene

waders get they never lose that old dog smell when they are wet!

The choice of a proper boat is often determined by the water you intend to fish. I see more mistakes made here than in the selection of rods, lines, and other fishing stuff put together. It seems a boat is a family purchase and not just for the single purpose of fishing. Someone in the family wants to water ski and someone else wants a cabin so you can get out of the rain, not to mention how nice an indoor toilet would be for some in the family.

They run out and buy a boat and sure enough the family wagon just won't pull that much weight. Then you can add the cost of a new truck to the cost of a big boat that probably weighs so much it'll get stuck at the ramp.

A BOATS' GOTTA GET YOU WHERE YOUR GOIN',... ITS GOTTA STAY OUTTA YOUR WAY, WHEN YA GET THERE, AN' ITS'.... GOTTA KEEP THE WATER OUT!

You don't need a boat that you have to christen with a bottle of champagne. Look for a boat that has the option of rowing, that way you can always get home. Pick one with as little hardware as possible so you are not fouling your fly lines on every cast. As for the cabin, you can't fish well when the weather turns real ugly anyway. Just

LITTLEST DIAMONDS I'VE EVER SEEN!

try throwing a six-weight line in a gale to see what I mean. I took the kids to Disneyland and bought the wife a pair of diamond earrings in trade for the horsepower, cabin, and the toilet. I ended up with a twelve-foot boat that can fish two anglers and didn't require a diesel rig to pull.

Remember you can't fish more than two anglers out of a boat if you are casting. With two anglers you also want two anchors so you have the ability to anchor cross-wind. With two fishermen you will be able to put the wind at your back for better distance and you will find the wind won't be blowing your lines into each other. This ability will save you a lesson in the advantages of barbless hooks.

It is always nice to be able to stand up so I'm not big on fishing out of canoes.

Use the Trout Bum philosophy: if you are not having to work two jobs to pay for your boat and truck then you will have more time to fish, which will make you a better fisherman.

There is one more piece of equipment that is useful when those ☉★⌗! mindless, low-life crumbs, that have more money than sense, and no manners at all, hit the water on those bothersome jet skis.............There is a waiting period, however!

MOTORS: Getting from here to there!

IDIOT STICKS (oars)

The oldest and still most reliable means of locomotion. If you need instructions then you are probably part of the reason they got their name.

REAL MOTORS

Infernal combustion engines, these have in fact come a long way in recent years. What you pick here is pretty much dictated by your boat and local water conditions. Remember, at 45 miles per hour you are traveling too fast to see hatches or subtle feeding practices. In short, you're not fishing!

Even float tubes need a motor. Don't try and save a dime on your fins for your float tube or your catamaran. It is a must that you get fins that turn up in front. This will allow you to walk around on dry land. Well, sort of!

Turned-up toe

Make sure you get an ankle tether. This is so important that if you can't buy one, make one. You don't want to leave a fin in the sticky mud along the shallows.

25

There is an old saying "90% of the fish are caught by 10% of the fishermen." None of us were born with rods in our hands and the road to becoming a great fisherman is traveled in small steps. Every little trick, every observation, every piece of knowledge, individually might only increase your effectiveness by one-half of one percent. Over time as you pick up more of these and add them together they will start to make a big difference.

VESTS:

Vests come in two styles: a standard vest and a vest called a shortie. For a lake fisherman who wants to float tube, the shortie is the one to choose. This is because the short model keeps your pockets out of the water. If you do all your fishing from a boat, get the standard.

NOTE: If you've been at this a while you know not all fly boxes fit all vests. If you're just starting make sure you take your boxes with you when you pick out your vest or vice versa.

SHORTIE

VERY SEXY

STANDARD LENGTH

HATS:

The broader the brim, the better the protection, especially for your ears. A dark hat absorbs the light better so there is not glare from the underside of the brim. The downside is that in the summer they are much hotter. The coolest and lightest hats are made from straw, but if the weave isn't tight they let the sun shine through on to your sunglasses and after a day of fishing you start to see dots in front of your eyes.

Well...nothing is perfect.

27

LUCK ACCUMULATES ON YER HAT 'N VEST OVER TIME...BUT IT'LL DISSOLVE IN SOAP AN' WATER. A REAL TROUT BUM DOESN'T WASH HIS HAT OR VEST.

SUNGLASSES:

These are dual-purpose tools. First and foremost they protect your eyes from hooks. Even if you don't like sunglasses or don't wear prescription glasses, you should think about wearing something to protect your eyes.

Your sunglasses should be polarized as this is a tremendous advantage in sight-fishing. The clearer the water, the more important this becomes. Don't forget those little cord doodads that hold your glasses around your neck.

MAGNIFIERS:

Magnifiers, for those who need them, are a must when tying on small flies. I've personally tried them all. The best, bar none, are the ones stamped out of small Fresnel lenses. These are soft plastic and stick to the inside of your sunglasses with water. They look like a bifocal and come in several magnifications. They are light and you always have them without looking through a pocket or having to clip something on. A thousand years from now there won't be rocks, sand and silt at the bottom of our lakes. The bottom will be a carpet of forceps, flashlights, and sunglasses.

FLY BOXES:

I like the little 3x4-inch box. These boxes come in several colors so you can color-code your flies. Nymphs in one color, dries in another. I also have boxes, for each of the seasons, that have a small number of flies from each of the color-coded boxes. A waterproof marker labels each box with a little 1/2-inch Avery stick-on label. I take a piece of clear packaging tape, trim it a half-inch larger than the label and slap this over the label to protect it from moisture. I've never had one wear out.

FORCEPS:

Forceps are used mostly to remove hooks from small trout. It is advisable to get a hefty pair that is big enough to crimp barbs down. I like to leave the barbs on until I fish the flies as the flies stick better in the foam. This way when I open my box on a windy day, I don't watch half a dozen of my flies blow away.

TIPPET SPOOLS:

My tippet spools are arranged so that the core group, 4x, 5x, and 6x, are on one side of my vest and the rest on the other side.

LEADER WALLET :

This holds extra tapered leaders as well as older ones that I save for bass fishing.

NIPPERS:

Everyone knows what these are for. I didn't start carrying them until my dentist (who is also a fly fisherman and should understand) refused to sharpen my teeth again.

HOOK SHARPENER:

If your lake has a rocky shoreline or if you fish out of a boat, a hook sharpener is a must. No matter how careful you are, you will still make a bad cast that will clip a rock or the gunwale of the boat. You have to stop every time you do this and inspect your fly, resharpening when needed. Also, before I use them, I like to dress the point on larger flies like size 10 and above. Small flies seldom need this added care.

STOMACH PUMP:

I don't like to use this on every fish I catch, as I like to return fish with as little handling as possible. However, when fishing is tough and I can't figure things out in the first couple of hours, I will pump the stomach of the first fish to find out what it's been eating. You will find the stomach pump such a good educational tool that you should always have one. With time and experience, the pump will be used with less frequency.

LEADER STRAIGHTENER:

The friction produced by pulling a leader or tippet through the two leather pads of a leader straightener produces heat which takes the memory out of nylon. It also removes some of the shine so that new tippet material won't reflect as much light. It's a little thing that at times can give you an edge over very selective fish. The downside is that the heat slightly weakens the tippet or leader. It's not important unless you straighten your tippet several hundred times.

FLY DRYERS:

I use three fly-drying techniques. The first is built into most vests and that is the lamb's wool patch to hold flies until they dry naturally. This is the easiest and best, but the slowest. When the fish are rising and I don't want to take time to tie on another fly or I am down to my last pattern and I just can't wait the half hour it takes Mother Nature to do her stuff, I use a chamois drier. This is simply a couple of 2X3-inch chamois rectangles riveted together on one end with a hole punched through so they can be connected to a zinger. If you squeeze your fly between the sheets of chamois it sucks the water right out. It works very well especially if made from thick hide, like elk-hide chamois. If you have an old chamois laying around, go stick your tongue on it and you can feel it work.

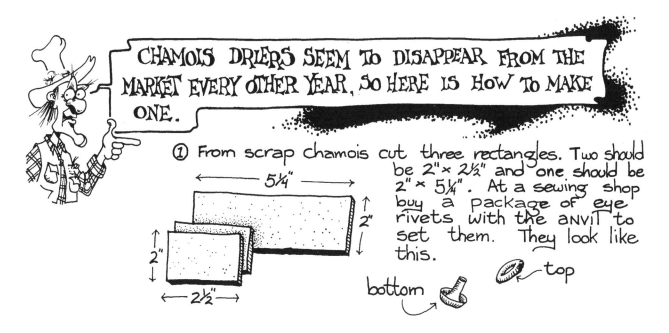

CHAMOIS DRIERS SEEM TO DISAPPEAR FROM THE MARKET EVERY OTHER YEAR, SO HERE IS HOW TO MAKE ONE.

① From scrap chamois cut three rectangles. Two should be 2" × 2½" and one should be 2" × 5¼". At a sewing shop buy a package of eye rivets with the anvil to set them. They look like this.

5¼"

2"

2"

2½"

bottom

top

The anvil has two parts, one of which you hit with a hammer. This will set the male end of the rivet into the female end. Once the rivet is set, notice there is a hole or eye that goes all the way through. Use this hole to attach your Zinger.

② Fold the long chamois piece over the two shorter ones and ...

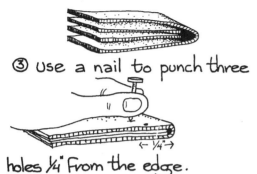

③ Use a nail to punch three

holes ¼" from the edge.

④ Put the male ends of the rivets through the holes and set the rivets. It's now ready to put on a Zinger.

IT WON'T WIN A BEAUTY CONTEST BUT IT'LL WORK SWELL. PUT IT INSIDE YOUR VEST TO PROTECT IT FROM LIGHT RAIN.

A real rainy day or a slip on a rock can turn your chamois into a water-logged wad of slime on a zinger. For times like these I use the last resort...dry-fly crystals. These crystals are about the size and texture of small-grained sand. They are made from the same material as the little beads you get in some products to absorb moisture. Dip a fly in these for a couple of seconds so it is covered and let it stand for a few more seconds. Then shake off all the crystals and it's ready for floatant. If you don't get all the crystals off they will absorb water into your fly at a very fast rate.

ZINGERS:

The old style of zinger had a spring-loaded reel held in place in a housing with a screw. Any of the small tools you used was clipped onto a cable or string that the spring would wind up on the spool. Maybe it was just bad luck, but the screw holding them together kept falling apart on me and I lost a lot of tools. A new zinger is available that has a spiral cord like a telephone. This cord just springs back into a cylindrical tube. I thought at first it might kink up like my phone cord, but after several years I have not lost tools or had to unravel any kinks. With no moving parts it is a good example of the K.I.S.S. principle. (Keep It Simple Stupid)

One more thought on zingers: I pin them to the inside of my vest so none of the most used tools are dangling out somewhere to foul in my fly line.

SPRING - LOADED ZINGER

PHONE CORD RETRACTOR

STRIKE INDICATORS:

The purists like to call these bobbers. In a perfect world trout would only feed on insects at the surface. But perfect it's not...And they don't.

IF IT WALKS LIKE A BOBBER AND IT TALKS LIKE A BOBBER THEN IT MUST BE A BOBBER!

THE SIMPLE FACT IS... THEY WORK !

Every year brings a new batch of strike indicators but a size 10 or 12 corkie, used in steelhead fishing, with a toothpick through it is an old standard that's affordable and hard to beat.

Another strike indicator that is adjustable can be made from hopper body foam from your fly shop. These are die cut and you feed your tippet material through with a sewing needle.

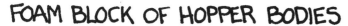

FOAM BLOCK OF HOPPER BODIES

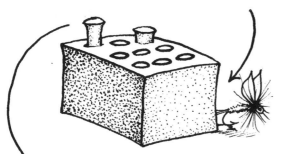

SEWING
NEEDLE WITH
TIPPET THREADED

FOAM BODY

THREAD YOUR TIPPET
THROUGH THE FOAM
SEVERAL TIMES, ENTERING
AND EXITING AT BOTH ENDS.

I carry needles in the foam in each of my fly boxes. Unlike the corky, if you step on them or crush the foam you don't break all your indicators. Simple friction holds it in place and you can slide it up and down without trying to remove a water-swollen toothpick stub.

FLY FLOATANT:

Again, just one won't work all the time. (There are several brands that melt at body temperature.) The reasoning is that a liquid will better soak into the fly. After the fly leaves your fingers the temperature drops and it turns back into a grease. These work real well until the weather gets into the 80s. Then it seems the floatant tends to wear off faster. At times like these I use a stiffer melting and stickier floatant. In the fall when the temperature drops I go back to the easy melt floatant.

FLASHLIGHT:

Here is an often misunderstood piece of equipment. Each year's new flashlight is stronger and brighter. Soon you will have the

34

equivalent in candle power of an off-shore lighthouse, able to burn your retinas out. The less light you can fish with, the easier it is on your eyes. My poor flashlight in my vest is made of plastic, holds only one AA battery and puts out about as much light as a cigarette lighter. I will say this much for my flashlight, when it's turned off it doesn't take twenty minutes for my eyes to readjust to the dark. The plastic is also more comfortable than the nice metal ones when you're holding it between your teeth. In my float tube, I carry a flashlight that cavers and rock climbers use, with a head strap and battery pack in the back. With this, whichever way I turn my head, the light shines. I don't really use this for fishing but for hiking out from lakes in the dark. This frees up my hands to carry equipment, fight the bushes and to catch me when I fall. It has been a big help!

MONOCULAR:

This is half a binocular. Mine is adjustable to focus as close as 12 feet.   It has been very useful for identifying hatches that seem to be just out of visual range. Since I've only got one good eye, a small binocular is one system of lenses too many.

NETS:

There are a lot to chose from but for float tubing look for a folding net made by Gudebrod that is so compact it fits on the inside of my vest. It has cotton mesh so it does a minimum of damage to the fish and never gets hung up. It won't win any beauty contests, nor is the handle long enough for a good boat net, but for function it can't be beat.

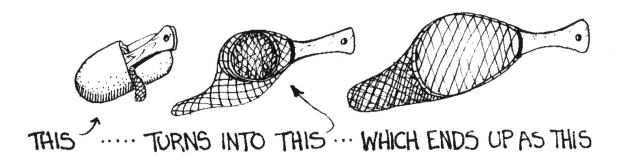

THIS ·····> TURNS INTO THIS ··· WHICH ENDS UP AS THIS

BOAT BAG:

Here I carry extra stuff as well as little-used stuff like spools, fly boxes, a Leatherman and Swiss-style army knife and, if I bother, a sandwich and candy bar. Sealed away is a bottle of insect repellent. It's sealed because the Deet (the active ingredient that chases away bugs) will eat up a fly line and ruin it. If I go out into the lake in a float tube, I'll carefully empty the contents of my boat bag into the storage compartments on the tube, keeping my fly boxes on top and in front.

There are a few other goodies that are helpful but I can only stand so much shopping...Even if it is for fly-fishing stuff. Now that we have an arsenal better than most third world countries, we need to start thinking about fishing.

The lakes we fish come in all sizes and shapes, from beaver ponds to an almost ocean, like Lake Superior. Success in stillwater fishing means learning where the fish should be found and why they are there.

Water has a couple of unique features that, once understood, will go a long way in improving your fishing. Water is the heaviest at 39 degrees. This means in the winter, water colder than 39 degrees will float on top. It also means that in the summer, water warmer than 39 degrees will also float on top of the cold, dense layer. Only twice a year, once in the spring after ice-out and once in the fall before freezing, is the lake a uniform temperature. These are those mysterious periods referred to around fly shops as "turn over." During these times the winds are able to generate slight currents that suck water up from the up-wind side of the lake, and pile water on the down-wind side of the lake which causes a circular current bringing the water from the bottom to the top. This current carries nutrients from the bottom of the lake to the surface, to be absorbed and used by plants and micro-critters. It also takes oxygen from the

At "turn over" the lake has a uniform temperature with no thermocline. Water from the surface can circulate to the bottom and vice versa.

38

surface to the bottom of the lake, and are the two times of the year when the fish can be found anywhere in the lake.

As the season moves along into spring and summer, the winds keep blowing and the current keeps flowing but the water starts to warm and the current, slight as it is, shears above the dense water and produces a thermocline. Most of us were taught that the temperature is the key to finding fish. What we weren't taught was that the oxygen levels are as important, if not more so, than the temperature.

Thermocline

The thermocline moves deeper during warmer weather, like mid-summer, and shallower in the cooler months of fall

Although the thermocline may have the best temperature for the comfort of the fish, it does not have the oxygen levels to keep the fish below this zone.

There is an area below the thermocline that develops during the summer months on moderate to large lakes called a chemocline.

Below the chemocline, which extends to the bottom of the lake, oxygen is even harder to find and in some lakes this is almost a dead zone, unable to support fish life.

THE THERMOCLINE IS LOW IN OXYGEN SO I LIKE TO SPEND MY SUMMERS RIGHT ABOVE IT. SNEAKING TO THE SURFACE FOR A MEAL, NOW AND AGAIN.

BELOW THE CHEMOCLINE THERE'S EVEN LESS OXYGEN! I JUST CAN'T LAST LONG DOWN HERE UNLESS THERE'S AN UNDERWATER SPRING.

In beaver ponds and shallow lakes these phenomenon may not appear. In lakes way down south it may be warm enough that there is no winter and spring turnover. Look at your conditions and decide if it applies. Just like people, the moods and personalities of a lake change with the seasons. Part of the fun is discovering how they change.

THIS CUTAWAY OF A LAKE SHOWS WHERE FISH SPEND MOST OF THEIR TIME. WHEN THEY START SHOWING UP OUTSIDE THIS AREA, PAY ATTENTION 'CAUSE THE LAKE IS GIVING UP ONE OF HER SECRETS.

FISH Hold in The SHADED AREAS

Now that we have some idea why and where fish hold in the center of the lake, we have to discover why they like to spend time along the shore.

HOW ABOUT FOOD?

Think of the shallows as a war zone. The fish come in like U-boats to prey on convoys of insects and minnows found in abundance along any shoreline. Overhead, the fish

41

are hunted by an air force of ospreys, eagles, kingfishers, blue herons, cormorants, and a half dozen or so fish ducks. Success means surviving for another day, and failure means they end up as a bird dropping along the shore. Keep in mind that the shallows are a dangerous and nervous place for the fish to be.

Like the convoys of W.W.II, there are areas in lakes where the insects congregate. Some insects prefer a special silt or sand bottom that is hard for an angler to discover. These areas are the special secrets that lakes don't reveal easily. There are areas along most shorelines that are more obvious and these are areas with...

SEAWEED

If you like speaking Latin you can call them "aquatic plants." Whatever you want to call them, seaweed comes in three types.

Seaweed that grows up in the air; these are cattails and bulrushes and such. These are the species found in the shallowest parts of a lake.

Seaweed that grows to the surface; the best known are water- lilies and they are found in the area between shallow plants and deep- water plants.

Lastly, is the seaweed that stays below the surface. These species can go as far down in the lake as the light will penetrate. During daylight hours these plants also put oxygen back in the water. This, along with cover, makes good habitat for insect and aquatic critter growth.

A large fish that bolts through any of these areas usually wins its freedom. Fine tippets and coarse seaweed don't mix. As a result most fishing happens along the edges of the various kinds of seaweed with the eventual outcome relying on a certain amount of luck.

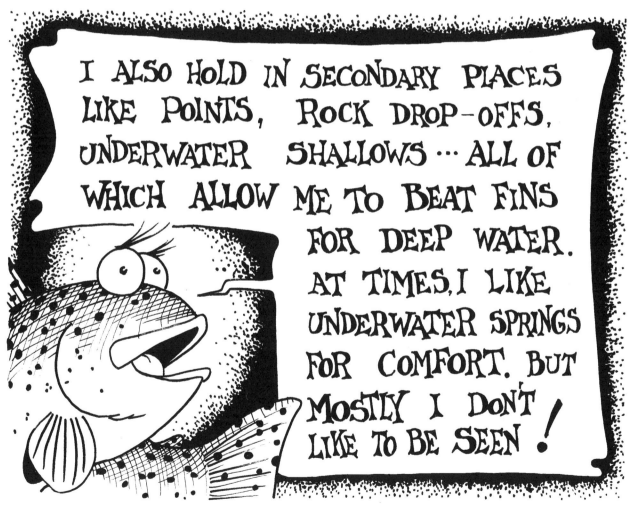

I ALSO HOLD IN SECONDARY PLACES LIKE POINTS, ROCK DROP-OFFS, UNDERWATER SHALLOWS ··· ALL OF WHICH ALLOW ME TO BEAT FINS FOR DEEP WATER. AT TIMES, I LIKE UNDERWATER SPRINGS FOR COMFORT. BUT MOSTLY I DON'T LIKE TO BE SEEN !

What appears to us as a nice, serene, friendly lake is an environment that is in a state of flux throughout the season. Temperatures and oxygen content can fluctuate from ideal to lethal in some waters. If you are new to stillwater fishing there are three techniques you must learn:

THE THREE MOST IMPORTANT FISH-CATCHING TECHNIQUES ARE: OBSERVE, OBSERVE, AND LASTLY ..... OBSERVE !

Now I'm not talking about just observing bugs. Entomology is the most important, but not the only, element you need keep an eye on. The fisherman who wants to become a master will monitor a great many things.

Let's start with the weather. You need to observe the weather on both a large and a small scale. The large scale is, of course, the seasons. The seasons will af- fect the timing of hatches. A long winter and a cold spring will delay the hatches from two weeks to as much as a month. A warm winter and a warm spring will accelerate the whole hatching process. Don't assume that because you did well on the 15th of June last year that it will be the same fishing on the 15th of June this year. A fishing journal is good for tracking the weather (as well as hatches and other things). Don't trust your memory, after a few years you'll get confused.

WAS THAT HATCH IN JUNE OR JULY? DAD BURN IF I'D JUST WRITTEN IT DOWN!

The weather, on a smaller scale, should be monitored by keeping track of changes the week before you go to your lake and daily while you are there. Like the seasons, a cold week before your fishing trip will have an adverse effect on the hatches. Some insects like to hatch under different daily conditions, some like sunny days, and some like overcast and humid days. Most insects have a favorite time of day in which they come out to play. Don't ask me how a bug at the bottom of a lake with a brain the size of a grain of sand can tell what the weather is like up above, because I just don't know. These are all things to note in your journal. In a couple of seasons you will be much better at predicting the timing of hatches. This will translate into catching more fish.

Remember that each lake will be different and part of the fun of stillwater fishing is learning what kind of "spirit" each lake has.

Lakes, ponds, and marshes are not forever. It is in the nature of geology to fill in these little jewels and eventually destroy them. At some point, pick up a geology book and discover how rivers, glaciers and geologic up-thrusting produces lakes and ponds. Also read the sections on how lakes evolve into marshes and are eventually destroyed. Being able to visualize the life cycle of your lake will make your guesses as to depth, temperature and bottom conditions more accurate. A good rule of thumb is to view the surrounding geology; what is happening above the water will usually extend below the water. A rock outcropping that sticks out into a lake will produce a point. If the banks of the point are steep, then the point usually drops off into the lake at a steep angle. A gully will usually extend out into the lake and produce a deep hole.

Shallow lakes are usually found in flat or low hill environments. Lakes produced by the change in a river's course will never be deeper than the parent river. Most lakes eventually fill in and certain sediment and shallow areas can be found in front of some feeder streams. This sediment can be favored by certain species of insects. This will often make that part of the lake more productive at certain times of the year. When you discover one of your lake's secrets, note it down in your journal, as it may reflect a condition that exists on other lakes in you area.

JUST LIKE PLAYING MONOPOLY...THERE'S GOOD REAL ESTATE AND THERE'S NOT SO GOOD REAL ESTATE

No other animal, except the fish themselves, will tell you more about a lake than the birds. Eagles and ospreys hunt the open deeper

LOOK...I FISH BARBLESS TOO!

water and are good at catching medium to large trout. In lakes that have populations of these birds you can bet that there are fish ten inches and over. They don't like the shallows much because it is a good place to bust a wing diving for fish.

Blue herons and egrets work the shallows and are a good indicator of small to

AH, THERE GOES ME STRIKE INDICATOR!

medium-size fish.   These birds are shallow-water indicators only.

For an indicator of small fish look for kingfishers.   These work the surface water out to about fifty feet from shore. When you spot kingfishers it means that there is a breeding population of fish or a population of shiners that larger fish can feed upon.   Kingfishers usually mean you're in water suitable for streamers.

Grebes, mergansers, and cormorants are also found in numbers on lakes with a population of fish.

No single bird specializes in trout so you can't use the birds to separate trout from spiny ray waters.   You can, however, use the birds to tell relative sizes of fish.   Your monocular can come in handy for determining the species that the birds are feeding on ... if you have the patience.

Swallows and nighthawks are a dead giveaway that a hatch is underway. There is very little wasted energy in nature so the birds skimming the water aren't doing it for exercise.   Keep in mind that the wind is blowing the insects downwind, so in your mind draw a line from the area that the birds are working up wind to where the birds stop working and you have the area where the hatch is originating.   Sometimes this is an area where fish are also rising.

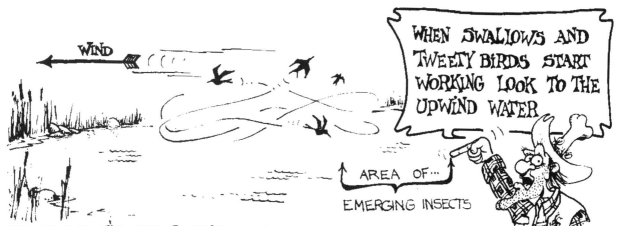

IF YOU DON'T SEE RISING FISH IT CAN MEAN THE FISH ARE FEEDING ON EMERGERS BEFORE THEY COME TO THE SURACE.

Birds aren't the only way to get a handle on what kind of bugs are out and about on your water. One of my favorite places to look is on the walls of the outhouse. It seems that a great many insects, besides blow flies, find there way in here.

49

Spiderwebs along the shore are worth looking for. As long as you are walking the shore, look at the cattails and bulrushes to see if anything is emerging. A bug net like you use in streams is good along the shore. Get a handful of grass, hold it in the water over the net, which I lay on the bottom, and shake it with enthusiasm. Pull the grass away and lift the net up and there are always a few critters that will give you clues to size and color. While you are there look under a few rocks and sticks to see if you can find leeches and scuds.

If you are camping, check the outside of your tent before you turn your lantern off. Like the outhouse, my tent seems to attract flies. I just hope it's for different reasons.

Every lake has a background color.

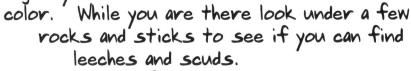

SEAWEED

NET

Lakes with a lot of algae appear to have a green cast while other lakes seem brown. Learn to observe the general color of the water and select flies to match. If there is no obvious hatch then this becomes even more important. If there are no rising fish then it means you must use a wet fly. In green lakes I select flies that are olive. In dark-brownish lakes with a high content of tannic acid you want to use browns and blacks. Insects that are going to survive and predominate in a lake are the ones whose color will blend in with the background.

When fish are showing on the surface you have the best indicator of where to fish. The dilemma for the fisherman is how to concentrate on the fly and still keep aware of everything that is going on around him. Many times I have caught myself concentrating on the mechanics of fishing to find that a massive hatch is underway and I've missed the first fifteen minutes. It's part of the game and it happens to us all. Train yourself to look around every few minutes, and fish with your ears as well as your eyes. Usually a fish rise is   unmistakable but they can do some funny things. I've seen trout shaking newly emergent damselflies out of the bulrushes. At first I mistook the fish for   muskrats or some other critter as they were in just a few inches of water.

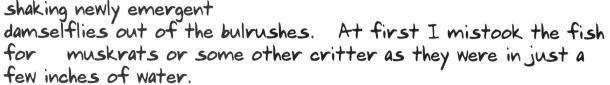

   Many bugs can emerge from their shucks in a few seconds. Great splashy rises usually indicate that this is happening. If the fish doesn't make contact with the emerger in a few seconds his meal is going to fly off. The lake is not a totally friendly environment for the fish and when they rise like this it means that they are giving away their presence, which they don't like to do.   When you see rises like this, start to look for the reason.

   Some insects spend a long time inflating their wings on the water. And at some point the females come back to lay their eggs. For mayflies this is called a spinner fall. Rises at these times can be little subtle surface slurps. At times you will see the nose, then the back and tail. These are my favorite rises because I can tell which direction the fish is traveling.

Remember not all rings and "V" wakes on the surface are from fish. A "V" wake can be caused by a little gust of wind. Salamanders, turtles, and some ducks can make rings on the surface. Most lakes produce methane gas from rotting stuff on the bottom. This means those bubbles you see are not all fish farts.

The single biggest mistake a stream fisherman makes in moving to a stillwater environment is assuming that the same flies which have become favorites on the river will work equally well on the lake. The following list shows ten of my favorite patterns for streams and ten of my favorite patterns for lakes in descending order of importance.

RIVERS   LAKES

1. Adams   1. Chironomid

2. Royal Wulff

3. Gold Ribbed Hare's Ear

4. March Brown

5. Pale Morning Dun

6. Yellow Stimulator

7. Tups Indispensible

8. Blue-Winged Olive

2. Woolly Bugger

3. Carey Special

4. Damsel Nymph

5. Compara Dun

6. Adams

7. Gold Ribbed Hare's Ear

8. Olive Soft Hackle

9. Elk Hair Caddis

9. Adult Damsel

10. Wool Head Sculpin

10. Wool Head Sculpin

Now don't pay attention to the individual flies because, unless you are fishing the same water at the same time that I am, your list will be different. Do pay attention to the fact that very few flies appear on both lists. What you have to do is start your own list. Now, it takes time but it's real simple. Your fish are going to eat the available food in your local waters. The larger the population of any given species the more of that particular species they are going to eat. The fish must consume more calories than they expend or they starve. Let's ignore the flies for awhile and concentrate on the bugs you can expect to find in your water.

LEARN TO NAME THE BUGS WITH ENGLISH NAMES. IT'S MORE EMBARRASSING TO GET SKUNKED IF YER SPEAKING LATIN !!

IDIOT !

54

here are four biggies when it comes to bugs for the fisherman: stoneflies, caddisflies, mayflies, and midges. There are also some others we will cover, but these four are the insects that most of the patterns duplicate. The big four are the ones most people have trouble with, as beetles, grasshoppers, and dragonflies are known to most of us by the third grade.

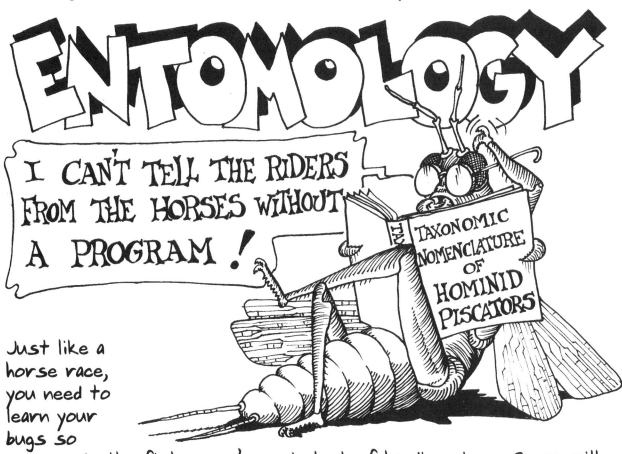

ENTOMOLOGY

I CAN'T TELL THE RIDERS FROM THE HORSES WITHOUT A PROGRAM !

TAXONOMIC NOMENCLATURE OF HOMINID PISCATORS

Just like a horse race, you need to learn your bugs so you can do the fisherman's equivalent of handicapping.   So we will start with the easiest, the stoneflies.   These belong to the order Plecoptera.   In the United States there are about 500 species.   These guys look like flying cockroaches.

What is nice about this order of insects for the Frogwater fisherman is...

YOU CAN FORGET 'EM !!

These ugly little guys live mostly in running water so they are very rare in lakes. The few species that live in lakes are found in the northern part of North America, but your chances of finding them in your water is about the same as finding a pegged-legged clam digger on a mud flat. On the off chance they make it into your water from a feeder stream, I'll show you how to spot them.

REMEMBER THIS !

1. THEY LOOK LIKE COCKROACHES.

2. THEY HAVE ANTENNAE ON BOTH ENDS...WELL, OK ONE SET ARE REALLY TAILS. BUT THEY LOOK THE SAME GOING OR COMING.

3. THE ADULT AND THE NYMPH LOOK ALIKE, BUT THE ADULT HAS FOUR WINGS.

4. AT REST, THE WINGS ARE FLAT ON TOP OF THE BODY.

Remember, if you find these guys you better check your map 'cause you just ain't at a lake; you've stumbled into a river.

There is one order of insect that is to fish what bread and butter is to us, or what grass is to cattle. This is the order of true flies called Diptera. All true flies have only two wings, which is the big identifying feature of these bugs. This order includes all the gnats, mosquitoes, black flies, deer flies, crane flies, and such. Lumped together there are about 3,500 species in this order that owe part of their existence to an aquatic environment. About 2000 of these species belong to the family Chironomidae. Around the lakes and fly shops these are chironomids. The adults look a lot like mosquitoes but they don't bite so are often ignored by most fly fishermen.

THE LIFE CYCLE OF THE MIDGE

The egg hatches into a....

LARVA ①

The larvae are known to fishermen as bloodworms.

Most larvae build a cocoon type of affair where they turn into a...

... PUPA ②

The pupae goes to the surface and in a few seconds emerges as an adult.

③
ADULT

The adults mate and then the female comes back and lays her eggs. The cycle starts all over again. Simple!

BLOODWORMS (MIDGE LARVA)

Now remember a few pages back we talked about the thermocline and the layer below it called a chemocline. If you were an insect, where in the lake would you want to live in order to escape from the fish? Yes! Right below the chemocline where there isn't very much oxygen. Down here you would have to adapt to the low oxygen content of the water, so lots of hemoglobin and a thin skin able to absorb oxygen would be assets. This is exactly what the bloodworms have done and how they got their color and their name. They do come in other colors but I only fuss with the red ones.

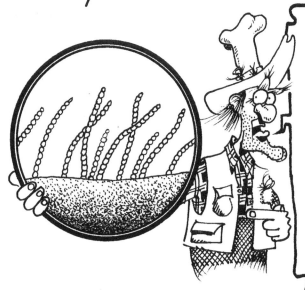

IN MY AQUARIUM AT HOME THEY WOULD STICK THEIR HEADS—OR MAYBE THEIR BUTTS—OUT OF THE MUD. IT'S KINDA HARD TO TELL ON WORMS!

Either way, they would wave in the water absorbing oxygen until you tapped on the glass. The slightest vibration and they would disappear into the mud in a heart beat.

Even with this advantage you can find bloodworms in the stomachs of trout. Maybe like oyster divers the trout hold their breath long enough to plunge below the chemocline for a quick snack. The lake levels, thermocline and chemocline are always moving, making bloodworms available at different times.

Bloodworms are represented by a pattern with the same name. The large species are about an inch long and about the diameter of a number 10 hook. Don't confuse the bloodworm pattern with a San Juan Worm as they are different critters.

BLOODWORM
(often tied on a bentshank hook)

*bloodworms look like worms but they are not. They can swim and wiggle twice as fast as the garden variety worm.

USING A STOMACH PUMP IS THE ONLY WAY YOU WILL FIND BLOODWORMS!

The bloodworm is not a popular pattern and is only found in the fly boxes of a few fishermen. The reason for this is simply that it is considered a worm pattern. There is a common prejudice against flies that duplicate goodies that are used by bait fishermen. The Bloodworm, San Juan Worm, and Glo Bugs all are better patterns than the fly-fishing community is willing to admit.

* One strength of this pattern is that it can be effective year around because bloodworms exist during all seasons.

* The red color gives this an added attractive value. At times, a red, orange, or chartreuse accent color will increase the effectiveness of any pattern. At some point, look up the flies used for reservoir fishing in Great Britain.

* To fish these, follow the directions for fishing the pupa.

The bloodworm will go through a metamorphosis and turn into a pupa. The pupa will, of course, turn into an adult. Unlike the bloodworm who can hide in unfriendly water, the pupa must run the gauntlet to the surface. This is the weakest link in the life cycle of the midge. This is also the one most targeted by fish and fishermen.

Midges, of one species or another, hatch out every day of the year unless the lake is frozen over. This means that even though the winter hatches aren't very big they do provide food for the fish during the lean seasons. Some scientist types even believe that trout couldn't exist in lakes if this order of insect were to suddenly disappear.

CHIRONOMID (MIDGE PUPA)

If you are to come away from this book learning only one thing, then let it be this section on the midge pupa. In some waters these account for three quarters of a fish's diet. "Chironomid" is the name you will find these flies under at your local fly shop. One other pattern called a "Brassie" is also a midge pupa pattern.

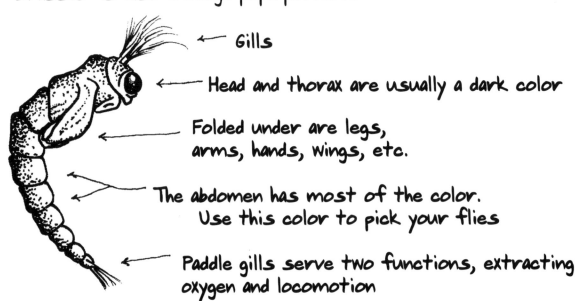

← Gills

← Head and thorax are usually a dark color

← Folded under are legs, arms, hands, wings, etc.

← The abdomen has most of the color. Use this color to pick your flies

← Paddle gills serve two functions, extracting oxygen and locomotion

★ CHIRONOMID FACTS ★

A few facts that are generally true about the midge pupa. Keep these in mind as we go through this section. Your local water most probably will show some variations of these facts. It's up to you to discover them.

✴   Chironomids are the most plentiful insect in most lakes.

✴   Multiple species exist side by side, so a pumped stomach will show chironomids of different colors. Choose your fly for the most common color found in the stomach.

✴   Midge pupae are larger the farther north you fish. Warmer southern water has several generations during a season so the little puppies don't take the time to grow like their northern relatives, who only hatch once per season.

✴   My most useful sizes are on 14, 16 and 18 hooks. But I carry these flies from size 22 through size 8.

✴   Olive and black are the two most common colors with tan, brown, and red running a close second.

✴   The take is almost always gentle, kinda like the fish just slurps them in. The fish is usually hooked right on the upper lip. I don't know why, but it's true more often than not.

There are two opinions on fishing chironomids: some love them...some don't. Many fishermen find them boring. I don't think they are boring but they are demanding. As I belong to the school that loves these little guys, I carry, at all times, two boxes full of them in all the above sizes and colors.

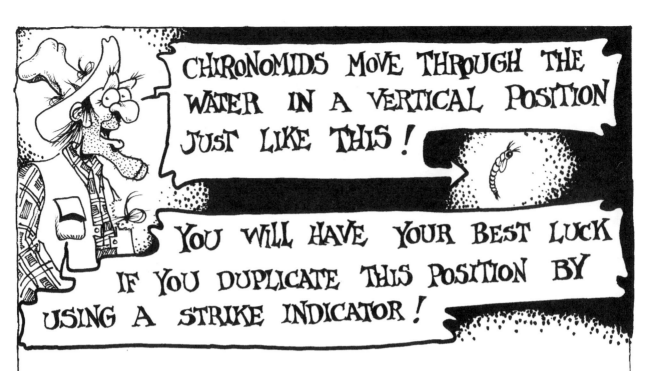

CHIRONOMIDS MOVE THROUGH THE WATER IN A VERTICAL POSITION JUST LIKE THIS!

YOU WILL HAVE YOUR BEST LUCK IF YOU DUPLICATE THIS POSITION BY USING A STRIKE INDICATOR!

Yes, you can catch fish using the normal nymphing techniques, with a dry line and no strike indicator, but not the lunkers on a regular basis. The standard nymphing techniques cause the fly to go through the water sideways during the retrieve. The big ones are sensitive to a natural presentation and will usually ignore a chironomid moving horizontally. This is what I recommend for shallow chironomid fishin'.

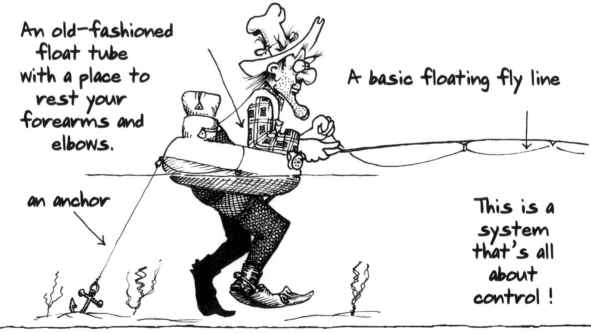

An old-fashioned float tube with a place to rest your forearms and elbows.

A basic floating fly line

an anchor

This is a system that's all about control!

Why an anchor?.... Since the chironomids move up and down, the slightest breeze will push you along at a good clip. This will cause the fly to come through the water sideways. We don't want that!

Why an arm rest?.... First, from an anchored float tube you can put your rod tip just under the surface of the water. This gets rid of the gravity belly and keeps you in better contact with the fly.

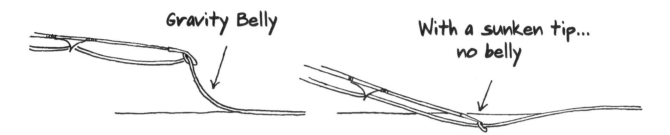

Gravity Belly

With a sunken tip...
no belly

Second, the sunken tip allows for a proper retrieval. As you retrieve the fly one inch at a time, any action is absorbed in the slack of the gravity belly.   This process is less tiring if you can rest your forearms on something.

To further keep in direct contact with your fly, try to always an-chor upwind of where you want to fish. This way your fly line won't be blowing around and carrying your fly sideways.   Do everything you can to remove every inch of slack line between you and your fly.   A savvy trout will take these flies very gently and may spit it out in a heartbeat.   Slack is your worst enemy and direct contact is your best friend.

OK! NOW LET'S PUT ON YOUR STRIKE INDICATOR

HINT: If you are using the little corkie strike indicator, you want to put your toothpick through the hole from the fly side and break off the point right at the hole. This means if you throw a trailing loop it won't have as much to snare it and foul your tippet.

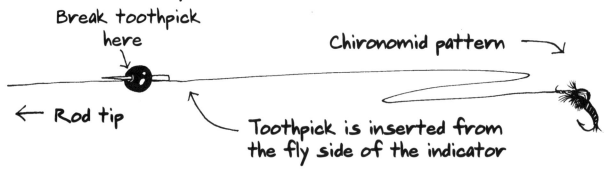

Break toothpick here

Chironomid pattern →

← Rod tip

Toothpick is inserted from the fly side of the indicator

If you use a hopper body indicator you don't have to worry about it, because nothing sticks out.

Adjust the tippet to the depth of the water. Since you will probably be fishing just outside of the weed beds, 12 to 24 inches is usually enough. Adjust your depth to be 10 to 14 inches off the bottom.

Try and place your fly so they will run right into it.

It oughtta look like this!

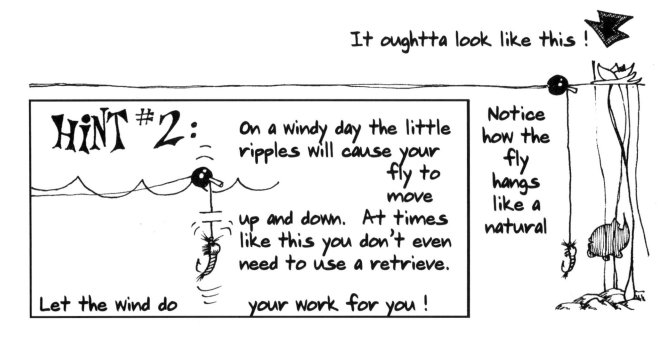

HINT #2: On a windy day the little ripples will cause your fly to move up and down. At times like this you don't even need to use a retrieve.

Let the wind do your work for you!

Notice how the fly hangs like a natural

Fishing these little puppies gets a lot harder when you get into deeper water. Deep water is any water deeper than the length of your rod. You can carefully stick your rod down and feel the bottom to determine the depth of the lake. Use this information to adjust your strike indicator. It works great even if your partners think you've lost your mind. When you can't feel the bottom then you must do two things:

The first is go to a longer tippet. But any tippet longer than your rod means you can't use a strike indicator that won't go through the guides on your rod.

So the second thing you have to do is go to a soft strike indicator. You make this out of Glo Bug yarn and nail knot it to your tippet. The beauty of this system is that this will reel right up through your guides. On occasion, when I am real desperate, I use tippets to 20 feet in length. These I couldn't cast but feed them out behind my float tube while I kicked along. Once the tippet was out I would drop my anchor and start fishing. Luckily these desperate days are few and far between.

If you find yourself needing to use this technique, then go slow and deliberate, or you will look like this.

LEARN MURPHY'S LAW OF CHRONOMID FISHING

Murphy's law of chironomid fishing states that your strike indicator won't go under until you look away. As long you're watching, it will just set on the surface .... ignored.

YET ANOTHER HINT: When you look away and then look back and can't find your strike indicator, set the hook. This is a common occurrence and you will miss a lot of fish if you are looking around too much. It's the fly fisherman's equivalent of shoot first and ask questions later.

These little critters come straight up to the surface wiggling their tails and, every once in a while, they stop to rest. Since they are heavier than water, when they rest they begin to sink. After a brief rest they will start wiggling to the surface again. Your retrieve has to reflect this.

With the rod tip under water start one-inch strips about a second apart.

PULL ····· PULL ····· PAUSE
VARY THE NUMBER OF PULLS. YOUR FLY WILL DO THIS.

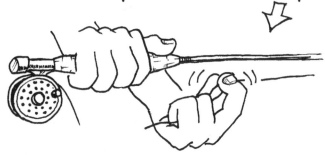

It should go like this:
PULL ····· PULL ····· PULL ····· PULL ····· PAUSE ·····

66

There are times you will want to fish down 2o to 30 feet just over the thermocline. Many midges can come from deep water. The best platform for this technique is a boat. Here you want to double anchor (a single-anchored boat will often swing in the wind). Any lateral drift will make a natural presentation impossible.

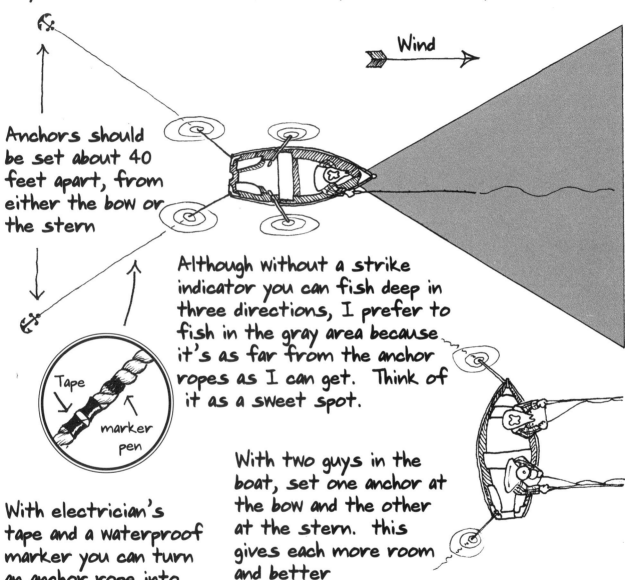

Wind

Anchors should be set about 40 feet apart, from either the bow or the stern

Tape
marker pen

Although without a strike indicator you can fish deep in three directions, I prefer to fish in the gray area because it's as far from the anchor ropes as I can get. Think of it as a sweet spot.

With electrician's tape and a waterproof marker you can turn an anchor rope into a depth sounder. One band of tape equals ten feet. A marker band equals five feet. This reads at 25 feet.

With two guys in the boat, set one anchor at the bow and the other at the stern. this gives each more room and better access to the downwind sweet spot.

If you fish with a southpaw arrange the seating so both rods are on the outside.

67

This is how to fish both the bloodworm and the chironomid. Also, it is a good way to search midday, midseason, when fish are holding above the thermocline, but not showing on the surface. It's important not to get in a hurry and it's important to fish from a stable platform, such as a boat. Like float-tube fishing, you can't swing around a lot or it will cause your fly to act in an unnatural manner. This is very effective if your lake is deep enough.

NOTE: Boat is at anchor.

After you cast your line let it drift down to almost vertical.

Count down your retrieve so when you find fish you can get back to the same depth

Each fly is equal to about one second of time, and one inch of movement.

Pause

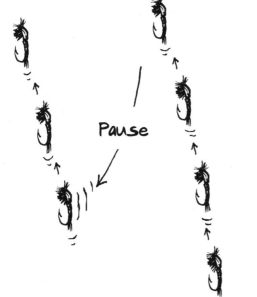

Keep your retreive to <u>one inch</u>

Remember your pause is as important as your pull.

After the pupa reaches the surface, its back splits open; the adult crawls out, inflates its wings, and flies off. As most of these are not biting insects the "emerger" phase often happens without the fisherman even knowing it has happened. Emerging is a very fast process and can be over in four or five seconds when the weather is warm, a little longer when it's cold.

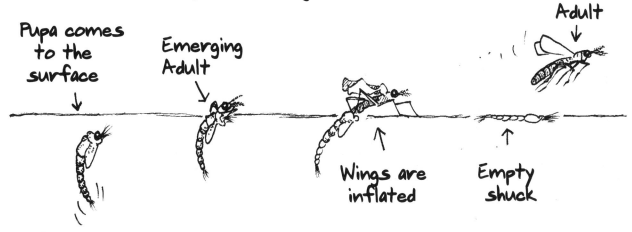

Pupa comes to the surface ↓

Emerging Adult ↓

Wings are inflated ↑

Empty shuck ↑

Adult ↓

There are several patterns that duplicate the emerger. Some have foam and some use CDC to float the fly in the surface film. Fish these patterns when you see fish working the surface. Often, right at dark is the largest hatch with the fish making real splashy rises. This is because with only four or five seconds before the adult is gone, the fish has to act fast or go hungry. This hatch is often confused with a Trico hatch but if you look close or shine a light on the water you will see empty cases floating on the surface.

Foam ball floats the fly and is easily seen

The emerger will float like a natural with the body hanging down below the surface film.

In my early days I would miss this because in the mad rush to find the right pattern, I wouldn't take the time to look at the surface film.   With age came wisdom and I now know what to look for and to stop for a minute to determine what is causing the fish frenzy.

the MIDGE ADULT

The four or five seconds it takes these little critters to emerge is about the only time they are accessible to the trout after the pupae reaches the surface.   Midges don't come back in big spinner falls like the mayflies, and I've never seen them flying low over the water like damselflies laying eggs. Not much is written about what they do after they leave the water.

The important time to target the adults are those few seconds when they are leaving the water.   With the right patterns you can have some of the best dry-fly fishing around. Traditionally the patterns that duplicate the midge are the Adams, Black Gnat, Mosquito, and the Griffith's Gnat.   But there are also Compara-Duns, and some standard ties like the Blue-Winged Olive, that can give you yeoman service.

70

Now, most species are just too small to duplicate, like the gnats, but on most water there is a midge that will come off in size 14 through size 10. (Up in Canada there are a few even bigger). These you can target with standard patterns. Match the color of the abdomen as best you can and cast to the rises. Let it set for a minute and if you don't get a strike then repeat the process on another rise. You want the fly to stay in the vicinity of the fish long enough for the fish to cruise its territory and see your fly.

Wing looks like →
fluttering wings

Body should be close to ↗
the natural

Tail looks like
a shuck

Again you are fishing standard dry-fly techniques, with a floating line, a 5X or 6X tippet. My favorite fly for this is the Compara-Dun with a body dubbed to match the color of the abdomen. And deer hair to match the color of the thorax.

In each population of adults there are a good number of midges that get stuck coming out of their shuck. I think it is their extra-long legs that get fouled, but I'm not sure. The important thing is how they act. Unable to free themselves, they buzz the surface of the water much like a seaplane dragging a parachute. They use a lot of energy but still remain on the surface film. They are an easy target for the fish. If this hatch happens just before dark when the birds are no longer a threat, I am convinced that the fish feed on these as a sort of game play.

Gently cast your fly in the direction you think the fish is going and retrieve it fast enough that it leaves a small wake. The strikes are so strong that you may find you need to go to a heavier tippet. If the midge is gray a standard mosquito will work.

Since this is the least addressed family of insects by the fly-tying community, good commercial patterns are hard to come by. Check your local fly shop. If they don't have what you need and you don't make your own flies, then take the following instructions to the nearest fly tier along with an adult specimen you are trying to duplicate. If you can't get hold of a fresh adult, then note these four characteristics.

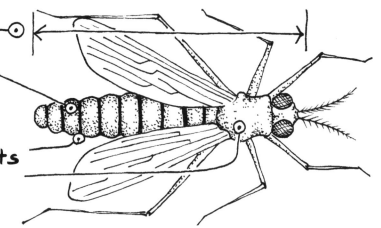

*  Overall length
* Color of abdoman

* Color between segments
* Color of thorax and wings

Most of us have enough stuff to carry so a ruler is a lot of added weight. Use you fingers and finger nails to measure as they are always handy (no pun intended) and hard to misplace.

Thumbnail ... 5/8 inch accross
Index finger ... one inch across

jet ski fingernail ... 1/2 inch across

Pinkie nail ... 3/8 inch across

You may want to tie the fly yourself. Here is a pattern—a system really—for tying a stillwater midge. With the four characteristics above you can imitate any midge on any lake. If you tie your own flies then make a quick trip to a weaving shop that handles some of the earthy colored wool yarns. I find that the most useful colors are tan, brown. gray, green, and pink. When the pattern calls for wool I use one strand of a three-strand hank ·········· It looks like this.

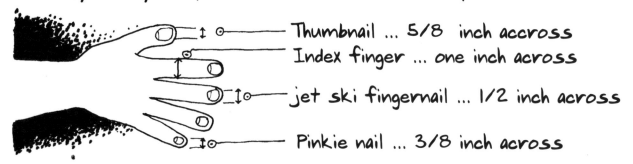

One
← strand

Stillwater Midge

Hook: 2x long shank, Dry-fly hook, 16-10
Thread: Black 8/0
Tail: One strand pearl Flashabou
Body: One strand twisted wool yarn
            to match the natural

Ribbing: 3/0 thread to match the
             natural
Wing: two light dun hackle tips
Wing case: Turkey to match the color
             of the natural's thorax
Thorax: Rabbit fur to match the
             natural

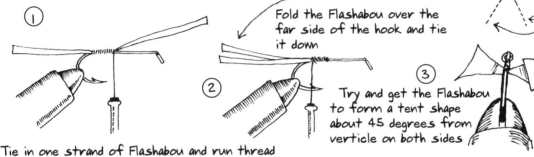

①

② Fold the Flashabou over the far side of the hook and tie it down

③ Try and get the Flashabou to form a tent shape about 45 degrees from verticle on both sides

Tie in one strand of Flashabou and run thread up the shank a little bit

The Flashabou will reflect light down at the same angle. What we want to acheive is a fly that will catch the attention of the fish long enough to make him key in on this bug and not all the others. From below, the Flashabou will look just like an empty shuck stuck on the back of a midge.

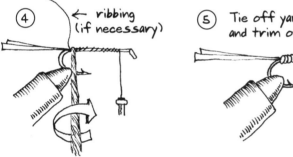

④ ← ribbing (if necessary)

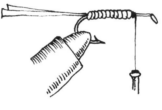

⑤ Tie off yarn and ribbing and trim off excess

⑥ Match turkey wing case to the natural

Twist the wool until it is very tight, then wrap body. Rib if the natural requires it

The wing case is used to keep the wings apart. The wings should be the lightest dun you can find and shorter than the body

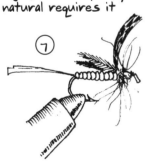

⑦

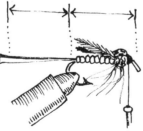

⑧ Trim the shuck tail to match the length of the fly

⑨ The finished fly as seen from above

Dub thorax to match the natural (usually gray or tan)—leave plenty of guard hairs for the legs

MOST ADULT MIDGES ARE GRAY OR TAN, WITH OTHERS IN OLIVE, BLACK, PINK, AN' GREEN

HERE ARE SOME USEFUL FLIES

Griffith's Gnat: This is a great pattern for those hatches of very small midges. You should have these from size 18 to size 22. Dead-drift your fly in the vicinity of rising fish and don't take your eyes off the fly. If you look away you'll never find it again.

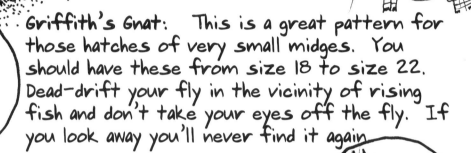

Black Gnat: This is useful in smaller sizes (14-18) for those hatches of black gnats or black flies. Dead-drift over rises.

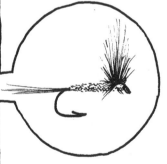

Compara-Dun: This only works for larger midges, size 16 and above. The advantage is it can often be found in the right colors at most good fly shops. Dead-drift it like the others.

Mosquito: This is a true midge pattern and can be used with good success in the right size for most midge hatches. Fish it like you would the Stillwater Midge.

Massive midday hatches are rare and usually occur on still, overcast days but evening hatches are a regular occurrence mid-summer through the fall. The midges won't reach the surface all over the lake at the same time. You might find an area has a heavy hatch but after twenty minutes or so the area of activity has moved a couple of hundred yards away. The rowing catamarans are the ideal platform for fishing this situation because you can move quickly to the new area and yet stay close enough to the surface to make sure the fish haven't switched to caddisflies or some other bug.

When you get on one of these hatches, fish a Stillwater or a mosquito in, or just under, the surface film so it wakes along, then hold on!!!

KEEP IN MIND THAT ONE REASON CHIRONOMIDS ARE SO EFFECTIVE IS THAT THEY ARE AVAILABLE YEAR AROUND .....LET'S LOOK AT ANOTHER YEAR-AROUND CRITTER.

DAMSELFLIES

Most adult damselflies prey on midges and other flying insects; as a result they are found just about everywhere. In some lakes they are a major insect group and a must for the frogwater fly fisherman. Unlike the midges there are only two phases of their life, the nymph stage and the adult. The nymph will hatch out in the fall, molting several times over the winter and early spring; then depending on the weather, it will emerge mid-spring as an adult. The adults can be found flying around until the first frosts in the fall.

the DAMSEL NYMPH

Notice how much the nymph looks like the adult

Like the adult the nymph has very large eyes

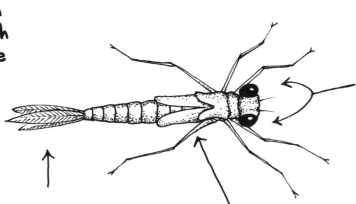

The gills or tail are very large and very feathery

The wing case extends about half the length of the body

They are usually found in lakes with a lot of aquatic plants, which makes them a much rarer find at high altitudes.

Most damselfly nymphs come in a very pale yellow-olive or a tannish brown color. Both colors are good camouflage when they are crawling around on aquatic plants. On occasion you will find them swimming around in open water. They don't look like they swim very well.

As they swim they keep their legs tucked underneath their body and wiggle back and forth in an exaggerated manner.

After they wiggle along for a foot or so, they usually stop and rest. Like most aquatic insects they are heavier than water so they sink very slowly while they rest.

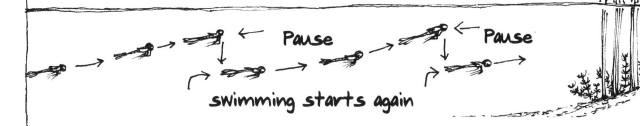

Pause   Pause

swimming starts again

Usually in spring the nymphs head for the cattails and bulrushes to hatch out into adults. At times, it is a huge migration. It's the best time during the year to fish the nymphs. If you find them climbing up on your float tube to emerge, it is a heavy hint on which pattern to fish. When this migration happens, try to fish your nymphs from deep to shallow water.

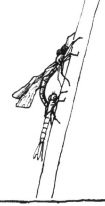

Unlike the chironomid, fishing the damsel nymph is pretty straightforward. A floating line will do well for shallow fishing, and a full-sink for getting deeper. Your retrieve is slightly faster than the retrieve for the chironomid.

The real challenge in fishing the damsel nymph is in duplicating the back-and-forth wiggle that is so typical of this nymph. There are two ways that I know how to do this. Old-timers used to slip a sequin, like they use in dress-making, up the tippet in front of the fly. It would act like a bill on a bass plug. When this was pulled through the water it would oscillate back and forth giving the fly the same action as the real nymph.

LIKE THIS

Standard damsel nymph

Small bead for a bearing

Tippet

Sequin

When this is pulled through the water it should look like this.

Although I've fished with an old-timer who used this technique, I have not fished it myself. You are on your own as to what size sequin to use.

The second technique will do the same but in a vertical plane and not a horizontal plane, unlike the original insect. These flies come in lots of different names, like Beadhead, Cyclops, and Goldheads. Whatever name they use they are basically the same.

The Goldhead Damsel

gold-plated brass bead

When stripping your line in small increments of two or three inches the heavy bead will cause the fly to dip down head first. This is much like the action of a small jig. With a pause now and again it will look somewhat like this in the water.

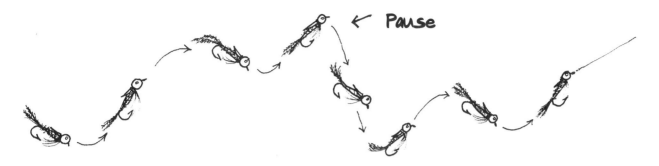

← Pause

It is somewhat like the natural but the movement is up and down and not sideways. The fish don't seem to notice the difference. There are days when the Beadhead will really turn the fish on. This technique is also simple, with no parts to lose, and the one I prefer.

Over weed beds and in shallow water you should use a standard damsel nymph that is unweighted. It will also sink like the natural. It just is impossible to give the fly the side-to-side swimming action of the natural. Beadhead flies will sink to the bottom too fast or drop into the weeds.

OLD CLASSIC TROUT PATTERNS ARE STILL AROUND FOR A REASON .... LIKE MAYBE THERE STILL GOOD !!

THE OL' ADULT DAMSELS

These handsome fellows are found from mid-spring to mid-fall on most lakes. On some waters their populations are huge. Most beginning fly fishermen overlook this insect. The flies for these guys have saved many a summer trip for me.

* Damsels are not good fliers on their first day as an adult.

* For the first day after they emerge they don't get their characteristic color.

* Damsels can fold their wings over their back and dragonflies hold their wings out to the side.

* Damselflies will rest along the shore on cattails and bulrushes when they are not mating or feeding.

Fishing the adult damsel is easier than finding the right fly. Large flies are notorious for twisting a fisherman's leader. Many are tied on huge hooks that are hard to float. Dragonflies will die spent wing, but all the damsels I've seen that died naturally have their wings back at about a 45 degree angle. Most trout target the head and thorax when they strike, just like saltwater fish target the eyes, so a small number 12 hook will do just fine. Not all patterns are created equal so spend time evaluating whatever you decide to throw at the trout.

PICKY PICKY PICKY

80

Now that you have a few flies, the most successful way to fish them is to find a shoreline with lots of cattails or bulrushes; from deep water, cast into the shore and dead-drift the fly. The take is usually a gentle slurp. Set the hook and the fish is on. You can twitch the fly every minute or so if you wish but let it lay still until all the water rings have disappeared.

On rare occasions a weather front will come through. Should you be out on the water when it starts to rain heavy or, better still, hail, many large insects, such as the adult damsels, will get knocked into the water. Keep an eye out for these special situations. The large fish know what is happening and try to take advantage of the circumstances.

DRAGONFLIES

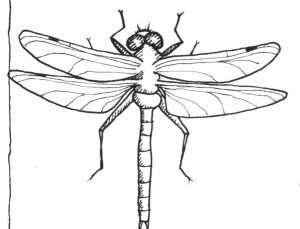

Note: These guys always rest and fly with their wings in what we call a spent wing fashion.

The adults are around during the summer and early fall months just like the damselflies.

The nymphs can take as long as three years before they mature enough to emerge as adults. This is real good news to a fly fisherman as there can be no mistake in the size of hook used on the imitation. Small hooks can represent one- and two-year nymphs and larger hooks, three- and four-year nymphs.

The nymphs come mostly in two basic shapes: short and dumpy, and long and streamlined.   Both are found close to the bottom or in weed beds.

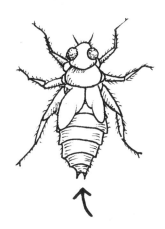

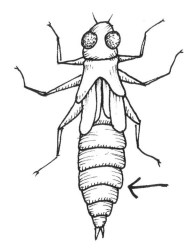

Long and sleek, this guy can get three inches long

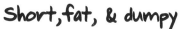

Short, fat, & dumpy

These are the top of the insect food chain in the lakes.   They are efficient predators able to catch and eat small fish, as well as each other.   The gills for these guys are inside their body and they can take in water, like filling a water balloon, and eject it out their butt.   This makes them a rocket-propelled bug. This ability is used to capture prey and escape from larger trout.   This super-fast escape trick is why most trout hit dragon patterns hard.

Fishing the nymphs is a year-round opportunity.   Unlike other species, size is not critical. At any given time there will be critters from different years and thus different sizes.   Unlike damsels, they are strictly targets of opportunity and are not sought out during a specific time of year. Each one is big enough to be a three-course meal, plus dessert, for the average trout.

When the nymphs are not jetting around they are creeping around the bottom or clinging to weeds. Think of them as underwater lions, slinking through the weeds in search of a meal with an occasional sprint to make a kill. Your retrieve should represent this activity.

You want to fish these close to shore, weed beds, or points as they are not found swimming around in open water. You also want to fish them close to the bottom or right on the bottom.   Vary your retrieve during daylight hours.

one of the most common ways to fish dragons is to...

...kick along the shore with a full-sinking line nice and slow-like. While I'm moving along I use my left hand to give the little jerks that bring the fly to life.
   Bringing the fly to life is one of the keys to becoming a better fisherman. You can do this with your fly selection.

MORE

THE FLY FISHERMAN'S "CATCH 22"
HERE ARE TWO FLIES YOU CAN FISH AS DRAGONS

THIS ONE LOOKS ALIVE BUT DOESN'T ACT ALIVE...

THIS ONE DOESN'T LOOK ALIVE BUT IT ACTS ALIVE.

The dilemma is action versus representation. It always has been and always will be a bone of contention between the various schools of fly fishermen. This gives us something besides politics to argue about all winter.

My take on this argument is that realistic flies usually sacrifice action. I want two things in the patterns I use. I want a fly that looks alive and when possible a fly that can represent more than one species. In the case of the dragonfly nymph I select patterns that can also represent leeches. Certain materials give the illusion of life in the water. Marabou, peacock, and pheasant are a couple of my favorite materials. One or more are used in my favorite patterns, the Woolly Bugger, Carey Special, and Jack Gartside's Sparrow.

EVERYONE'S GOT AN OPINION

84

SPEAKING OF LEECHES

Leeches aren't insects but I'm putting these right after the dragonflies because I use the same flies to target both of these groups. Don't think of leeches like they are portrayed in the old "African Queen" movie. True, some are bloodsuckers, but most live on a diet of rotting vegetable matter. Think of these guys as swimming worms. Just like worms, there are a few that are parasitic but most go about their lives making the garden a better place. They improve your fishing hole, if for no other reason than being an important food source for large trout.

There is a lot about leeches I don't know, like how and when they reproduce and how long they live. What I do know is that I find them everywhere. I've found them stuck under rocks on the smallest alpine streams and in ponds just over the dunes from the ocean. In the same water I've seen them from 1/4 inch to more than 4 inches long.

They swim with an up-and-down paddling motion, sometimes constricting and elongating their length as they go. As an aid to swimming, the back half of these critters are flattened into a kind of paddle. Usually they are found along the shore or close to the bottom, but on occasion I have seen them out in the middle in open water. They swim like this:

A swimming leech

Note: Fat butt

If we got together and designed a fish food for the fly fisherman we couldn't improve on the leech. It is the easiest of all the lake foods to fish properly.

* As it comes in all lengths from 1/4 inch to 4 inches you can't make a mistake on size. I usually pick something in the smaller range about one-inch-long overall, to start.

* Since I've seen leeches everywhere from open water to under the rocks on the shore, there is no place you can't fish your fly with confidence. Remember, however, there are usually more fish along the shorelines.

* The up-and-down swimming motion of the naturals is the easiest retrieve for the fly fisherman to duplicate.

* Leech patterns can be mistaken for dragonfly patterns so you have the bonus of a two-species fly.

REMEMBER THE FISH BUM'S LAW "MATCH YOUR FLY TO THE COLOR OF THE WATER"!

As you become more familiar with your lake you will learn the colors that are most effective. To start, match the general impression you get of the color of the lake (unless it is crystal clear). If your water is crystal clear then start with black. Ninety percent of my leech fishing is done with black and olive. The other ten percent is brown, maroon, and gray. This may vary with your local conditions so ask at your fly shop.

A Woolly Bugger is a good place to start but there are many patterns for leeches; I have fished most of them and have yet to find a bad leech pattern. Select your flies in size 10-4, long-shank hooks. The Goldhead Leeches will also swim in a more natural fashion if you can find the flies tied that way.

Here are some patterns to consider:

Standard Woolly Bugger (good in the shallows and over weed beds)

Beadhead Woolly Bugger (good in water deep enough to let the action work without snagging bottom)

Marabou Leech
A great daylight leech pattern. (The weighted version will do what the beadhead Woolly Bugger does by swimming in a natural manner.)

Mohair Leech
A great favorite in Canada. (If you plan a trip to B.C., don't forget to get a few of these in maroon.)

Carey Special

(An old favorite with a peacock or black wool body which duplicates both the olive or black of the natural.)

SCUDS

Here is another critter that is not a bonafide insect, but rather a small crustacean.

* All crustaceans have a substance called carotene in their shells that, when eaten by trout, will turn the trout's flesh pink. You can look down the throat of a trout at the base of their gill covers and if it is pink, and not white, then it means it is eating either scud, or crawdads. A catch-and-release fisherman doesn't have to cut one open to determine if it is pink-fleshed or not.

* Scuds lay their eggs mostly in the spring and summer months.

* Scuds are found in all parts of the lake, deep and shallow, although in the spring they are more common in the shallows.

* Scuds come in many sizes and several shades of color in the same body of water. Maximum size is about one inch long.

* On the bottom, scuds crawl around very slowly, but when they swim it is in an erratic manner, turning on their backs and on their sides, a lot like this...

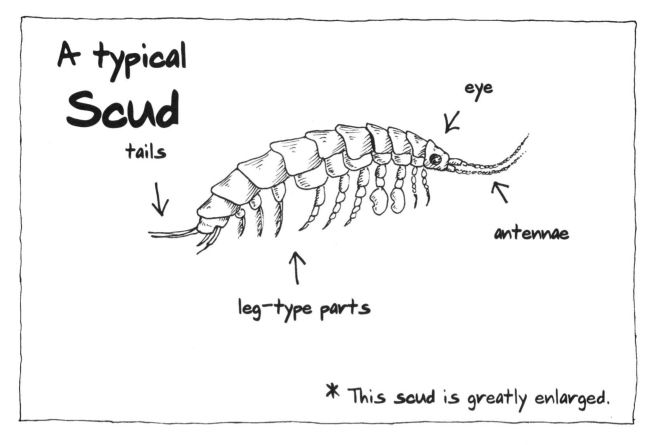

A typical
Scud

tails

eye

antennae

leg-type parts

*This **scud** is greatly enlarged.

Like the leech, the scud is another no-brainer to fish. Found in all parts of the lake, you can usually fish them anywhere at anytime. Size is also not critical as they can be found in many sizes in the same lake.

Your retrieve can be anywhere from dead-slow to fast and erratic.

On the lake, turn over some rocks or shake a handful of shore weeds in a bucket or pan and you should be able to find plenty of scuds to give you an idea on size and color.

PEOPLE NEVER NAME THEIR OWN FOOD AFTER AN IRAQI MISSILE!

Scuds and their patterns are usually found in tans, gingers, and light and dark olive.

Scud zones

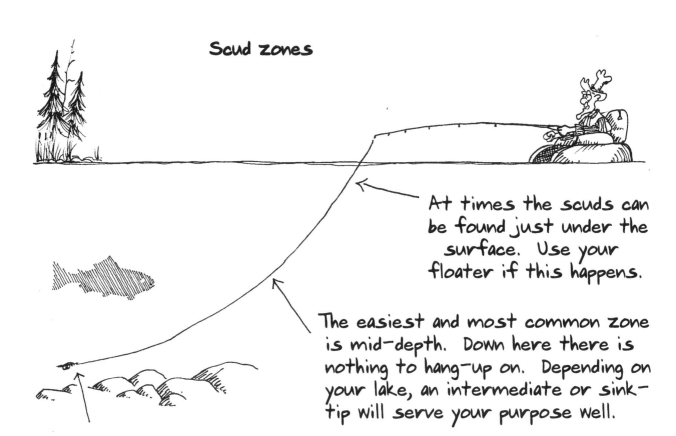

At times the scuds can be found just under the surface. Use your floater if this happens.

The easiest and most common zone is mid-depth. Down here there is nothing to hang-up on. Depending on your lake, an intermediate or sink-tip will serve your purpose well.

Hanging up and waiting for your fly to sink are the two problems with fishing the bottom. Here a slow retrieve is best to start with. If that doesn't work speed up your retrieve.

Scuds that have just molted are very light in color, almost white. Scuds that have gone off to scud heaven are often orange, kinda like a cooked shrimp. Generally tans and olives are your best bet, but at times white and orange will work miracles.

90

If you've turned over a few rocks in your lake and found scuds then you know they are present in several sizes. That's good news as you don't have to be as particular with hook sizes. These little fellows run from a size 20 to size 10.

When you pick out flies look for scuds tied on kind of straight hooks because the live ones look like this:

← live one

dead one

Some writers will tell you not to use orange as this is a color of the dead scud. They are right about it being the color of a dead scud but for some reason an orange scud can outperform other colors at times. Perhaps you have noticed, a trout will throw up its dinner after being hooked. It is not uncommon for fish traveling with it to pick up what is left of its dinner. It opens up a whole new area for fly tiers—partly digested, up-chuck patterns.

Nyerges Numph   R. K. Scud

Scud patterns can run from realistic like the R. K. Scud to simple impressionistic patterns like the Nyerges Nymph. Both work well. When you pick out your flies, start with the tan and olive colors in sizes 20 through size 10. Add a few of the bright-colored ones for those desperate days.

MAYFLIES

Mayflies are one of the big three insect orders in stream fishing and they are also big on lakes. Let's look at three species, one that is common and pretty representative of this order, and two that present special fishing opportunities. Before we do this we need to take a quick glance at a typical mayfly life cycle.

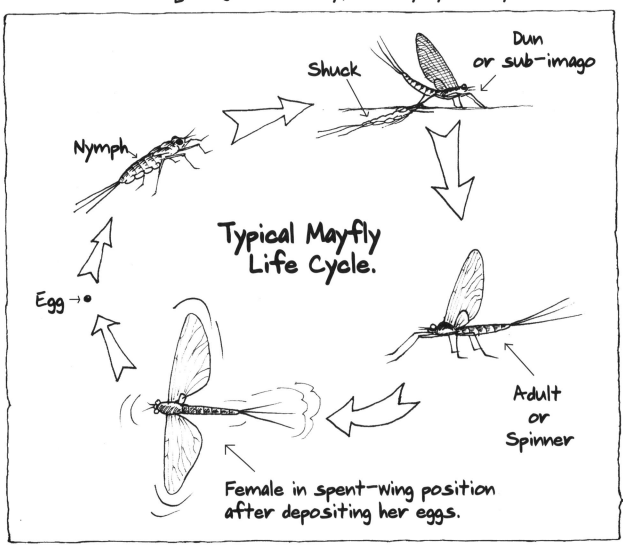

Nymph

Shuck

Dun or sub-imago

Typical Mayfly Life Cycle.

Egg →

Adult or Spinner

Female in spent-wing position after depositing her eggs.

No other insect group is as confusing as mayflies. Good old Mama Nature doesn't make very many mistakes, but for the life of me I can't figure out why she made a bug with two adult phases. (If you're one of those who thinks she can't make mistakes, go look up the duckbilled platypus.) I like to ponder just how this nutty system developed, but it remains one of fishing's many little unsolved mysteries.

Remember that duns are departing the water and spinners are coming back. The flies that imitate the different stages of the mayfly are a little confusing also.

* The nymph: The confusion here is that some nymphs are mistaken for stoneflies (remember that there are so few stoneflies in stillwater that we won't even cover them). The tails on the nymphs are what cause this confusion.

* The emerger: Imitates the nymph as it breaks out of its shuck to become a dun. These are fished right in the surface film.

* The dun: The coarser adult stage that leaves the water to molt into yet another more delicate adult form that is sexually mature.

* The cripple: Some mayflies have trouble emerging and hurt themselves. If a wing is damaged, then they are doomed and become easy pickings for a fish with an appetite.

* The spinner: After mating and egg-laying the female falls dead on the water. The flies are called spinners and some are called spent-wing flies. They make easy pickings!

Mayflies have a special place in the hearts of fly fishermen. It is a perfect insect to duplicate in fur and feather. Ephemeroptera is the scientific name for this order of bug. The name comes from ephemeral which means it lasts for a short time. This is largely because the adult stage doesn't eat or drink. The popularity of these insects means you have a great many flies that cover the various species and their different developmental phases.

FiSHiN' DA NYMPH

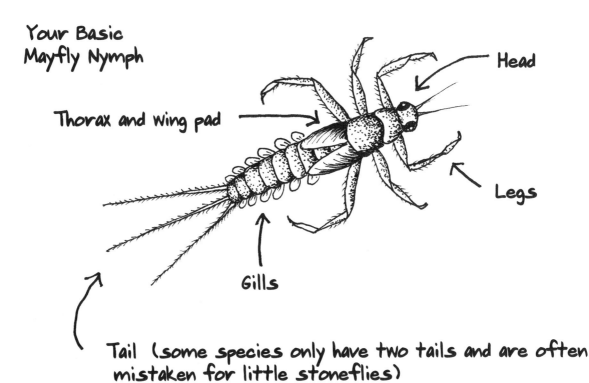

Your Basic
Mayfly Nymph

Head

Thorax and wing pad

Legs

Gills

Tail (some species only have two tails and are often mistaken for little stoneflies)

Most nymphs live along the bottom and in weed beds, but a few species burrow in the bottom silt. None of these guys make homes like the caddisflies. I have seen mayflies emerging from the middle of a lake, so as long as the hatch isn't happening, you want to fish your nymphs close to the bottom or alongside weed beds.

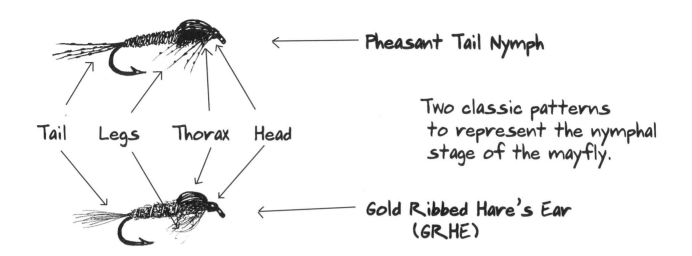

Pheasant Tail Nymph

Tail   Legs   Thorax   Head

Two classic patterns to represent the nymphal stage of the mayfly.

Gold Ribbed Hare's Ear (GRHE)

Although capable of swimming almost as fast as a small minnow these little puppies usually crawl slowly along the bottom until it's time to hatch. Then they will make for the surface.

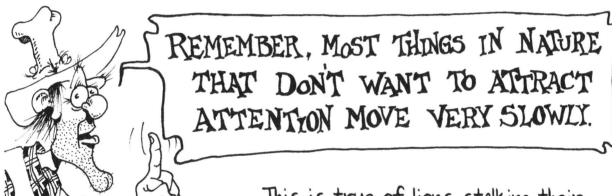

REMEMBER, MOST THINGS IN NATURE THAT DON'T WANT TO ATTRACT ATTENTION MOVE VERY SLOWLY.

This is true of lions stalking their prey and it's true of nymphs trying to hide from trout. Your retrieve should reflect this condition. If possible, on a slow day, catch a couple of these critters and study them so that you can better copy the speed and movements of the naturals.

Your retrieve should be a little faster than the one for Chironomids but still on the slow side. It is advantageous to do a couple of quick escaping strips every three or four feet. This will sometimes tease the trout into striking.   Try it and see.

95

Most of the nymphs are fished the same regardless of species. If you are out and see a nice hatch of duns coming off the water but no fish are working them, keep fishing the nymphs. On a few occasions the fish prefer to work the hatch from the bottom and not the top. If you find this happening, stick with the nymph until you see surface activity.

OK! LET'S TAKE A GANDER AT THREE MAYFLY SPECIES... ...THE GOOD, THE BAD AND THE UGLY!

Let's start with the good. This is the family of Callibaetis mayflies. There are several things that make these good. First they are widespread and common, found in a lot of stillwater. Second, they keep banker's hours. The duns come off from ten in the morning to two in the afternoon. This means that you don't have to be up before the chickens. They even give you enough time for breakfast. Did I mention, the trout love'm.

Common name: Speckle-wing Quill

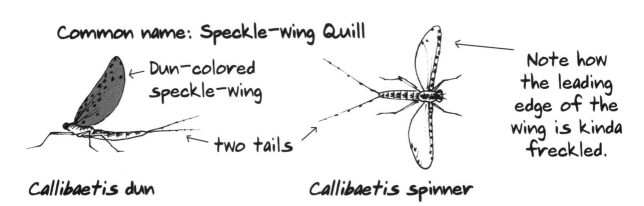

← Dun-colored speckle-wing

← two tails

Note how the leading edge of the wing is kinda freckled.

Callibaetis dun

Callibaetis spinner

Now I know some of you won't have *Callibaetis* in your lakes but you probably will have a similar mid-sized mayfly that will emerge midday. All the principles are the same. Your fly shop will name your mayfly and suggest patterns.

HINT: WHEN PICKING DRY FLY PATTERNS ALWAYS MATCH THE COLOR OF THE BUGS BELLY AN' NOT IT'S BACK. THE FISH ONLY SEES THE BELLY! OFTEN THEY ARE TWO DIFFERENT COLORS. A WHOLE LOTTA FLIES ARE TIED TO MATCH THE BACK... ...BEWARE!

One more word on color. Mayflies of the same species can come in different shades even in lakes only a few miles apart. If you tie your own flies then you can match each lake system perfectly. Take our old friend the *Callibaetis*, they come in light gray, olive-gray, and light tannish brown on three lakes I like to fish. When you hear anglers arguing about which color is exact for any given species, remember that there is always a lot of variation from lake to lake, and between the dun and spinner stage, as well.

Unless you live on a lake and can monitor hatches on a daily basis you have to drive and sometimes camp on the shore. Your first day at the lake must be, in part, a reconnoitring day.

Usually, on day one, your fist indication that a hatch is happening is when the trout start to take the duns. This is good news and bad news. The good news is that you are in for an hour of good dry-fly fishing. The bad news is that you missed the good nymph fishing just before the duns started showing.

Eighty percent of the time the hatch will happen at the same time on the second day. Why eighty percent of the time?

STATISTICALLY ···
TOMORROW'S WEATHER
HAS AN EIGHTY PERCENT
CHANCE OF BEING THE
SAME AS TODAY'S.

As long as the weather is the same then an hour before the duns emerge you want to fish a deep nymph on the way to the surface. With a twelve-foot leader cast out and let your fly sink until it is close to the bottom. Use a moderately fast retrieve to duplicate a nymph coming to the surface.

Floating fly line

Use this technique where you saw fish rising on your first day at the lake. Keep this up until the duns start to show and fish start to target them instead of the nymph.

Dry flies are always more fun than wet flies because you can watch the strike. When the fish start to target the duns, stop and redress your leader to within a foot of your fly. Dress your dry fly while you're at it.

Water Surface   Fly line

Undressed tippet just below the surface.

Stillwater trout have all the time in the world to examine your fly. Your dry flies should be much closer to the size and color of the original than you would use in a rolling river. This is why a lake fisherman seldom has attractor-type patterns like Royal Wulffs and Humpies in his fly box.

After you've changed to a dry, move out to where you are within range of working trout. I try to determine the direction the fish are moving with each rise and place my fly about six feet in front of the nearest rise. Don't try to hit the rings dead center. Let the fish come to the fly.

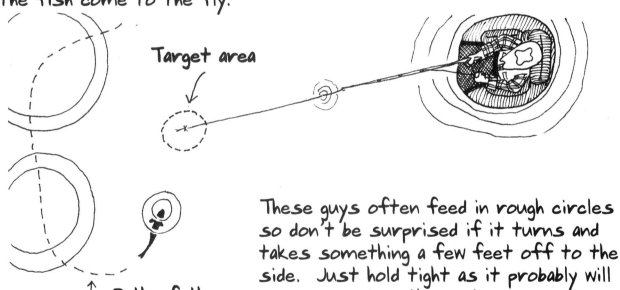

Target area

Path of the trout

These guys often feed in rough circles so don't be surprised if it turns and takes something a few feet off to the side. Just hold tight as it probably will come around on the next pass.

Try to concentrate on a delicate presentation and don't overcast. Whipping the water can put the fish down. If you make a bad cast, fish it out anyway as you are still probably in the fish's territory.

Every ten minutes or so look around to see what is happening on the entire lake. You may have rolling hatches. These are hatches that start at one point in the lake and move off to another as the day progresses. It will help you position yourself on the second day.

I don't know how, but the fish seem to know when and where things are going to happen. If a wind is blowing, the fish know that the duns and cripples are going to pile up on the downwind shore. You should be there too.

Wind direction

It's always nicer to cast downwind.

Few bugs will be found downwind of obstructions, they pile up just upwind from any stuff that sticks out from the water.

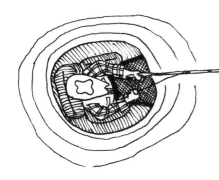

If you see the fish cruising, lead them by six feet or so just like in the open water.

Oftentimes the fish will swim back and forth slurping in front of any obstruction, usually only a foot away. Again, show a little patience. It is not uncommon for your fly to be passed up a time or two, but sooner or later it will get smacked.

When there are lots of mayflies on the surface, catch a couple and double check that their underside is the same color as your imitation. Double check size. If you are having trouble go to a finer tippet, something along the lines of a 6X.

A special situation happens often enough that I just gotta mention it. At times you will get strikes and when you set the hook find nothing is there. What is happening is that the fish will cause a vortex or whirlpool that pulls the fly under. The fish then swings around and a few seconds later swallows what he thinks is a mayfly. I really think it's a kind of play activity. Actually, trout will do this to caddis and midges as well. Should this start happening to you there are two things you can do:

The first thing is:

Wait the couple of seconds it takes the fish to find the fly, do not strike until you **feel** the fish.

If you are like me and have spent a lifetime honing your reflexes to the point that you are able to strike instantaneously with the power and accuracy of a king cobra, then the wait can be kinda hard.

OH BROTHER... WHAT A CROCK!

The more excited you get, the harder it is to wait those few seconds.

The second system I gleaned out of a book by Dave Hughes. He suggested using a pattern called a Hare's Ear. This should not be confused with the Gold Ribbed Hare's Ear. They have the same type of body but the Hare's Ear has the addition of a traditional wet-fly wing. This wet fly wing folds back much like the dark dun wing of the natural under the water. This trick has worked so well that I have tied wet-fly versions of all my lake mayflies, midges, and caddisflies.

Wing helps duplicate a drowning natural.

Hare's Ear

Body is about the same as a Gold Ribbed Hare's Ear except the tail is much more delicate, like the dun.

It is common to have trout suck the mayflies under water with their tail and then come around and pick them up with their mouth. If you are setting on takes, but not connecting, you know that the fish are drowning the mayflies first. This is the time to use these wet flies. Remember that the fish is circling trying to find the poor bug it just sucked under. The take will usually happen in just a couple of seconds. Cast your fly right into the rise and just let it settle, after a few seconds start a slow retrieve.

Hint: Move fast and get your fly in the ring quickly....

...before the fish quits lookin' an' moves on.

Note: This technique will work well during most *Callibaetis* hatches but is not quite as much fun as fishing a dry because you don't see the strike.

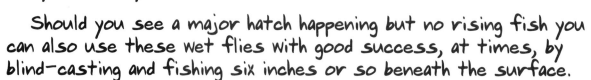

Should you see a major hatch happening but no rising fish you can also use these wet flies with good success, at times, by blind-casting and fishing six inches or so beneath the surface.

The *Callibaetis* has multiple generations per year. This means the nymphs that winter-over emerge in early spring. They lay eggs that hatch out and four or five weeks later they emerge. The eggs that the second group lays hatch, but as the days are getting shorter they are forced to emerge quickly. The third-generation nymphs winter-over until the next spring. Altogether there are three generations in a summer. The nymphs that winter-over are the biggest. Every generation after this one is about one hook size smaller. If you find your dream lake and go back the next month to find all your flies are too big, believe me you are not losing your mind. As a rule of thumb, after midsummer the size of the flies start getting smaller.

There are tons of patterns for the *Callibaetis* but to simplify things, these are four of the best. Even though they are not the fanciest, you can find them in any fly shop.

Gold Ribbed   Hare's Ear   Adams   Compara-Dun
Hare's Ear

Gold Ribbed Hare's Ear: Not only can this be fished as a nymph but
                 it can be dressed and fished just below or in the
                 surface film as an emerger. Natural, gray, or
                 gray-olive and tannish brown are the major colors.

Hare's Ear: Fish as instructed above. Don't ignore this fly or
                 the techniques (Thank you Mr. Dave Hughes).

Adams: This is a classic from the twenties and works
                 very well during a *Callibaetis* hatch. It can also be
                 mistaken for an adult midge and you know what I think
                 about flies that duplicate more than one species.
                         I love'm!

Compara-Dun: Lastly, this fly can be used to duplicate a *Callibaetis* in the emerger, dun, and spinner stages. Like the Adams it can also represent a midge.

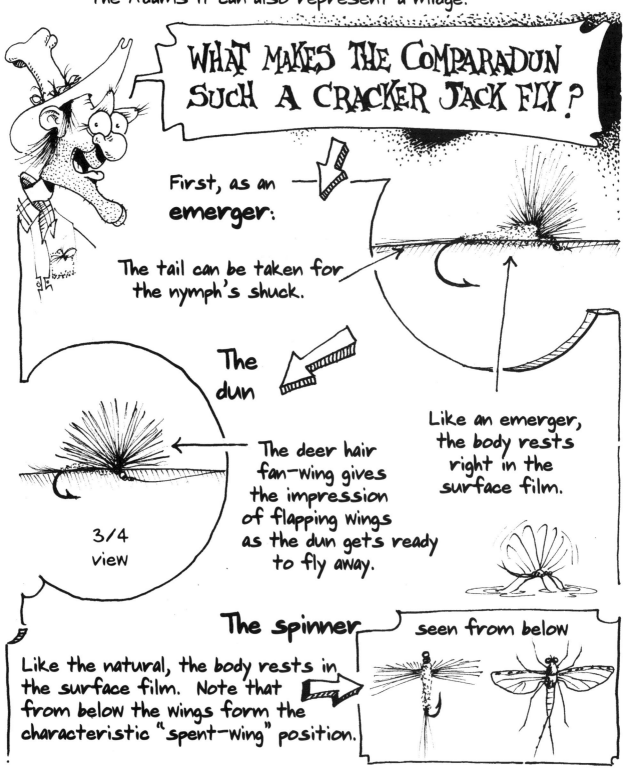

WHAT MAKES THE COMPARADUN SUCH A CRACKER JACK FLY?

First, as an **emerger:**

The tail can be taken for the nymph's shuck.

Like an emerger, the body rests right in the surface film.

The dun

The deer hair fan-wing gives the impression of flapping wings as the dun gets ready to fly away.

3/4 view

The spinner

seen from below

Like the natural, the body rests in the surface film. Note that from below the wings form the characteristic "spent-wing" position.

Hold on to your shorts because for stillwater fishing Compara-Duns can be tied with different body colors and using the new dyed deer hair, with different colored wings, as well. If you tie your own flies you don't have to buy expensive necks to make dynamite flies. If you are not yet tying your own flies, when you go to buy them, they often look like this.

Note: wing bent forward

Some fly tiers will tell you:

I TIE'M THIS WAY, SO AS THE WING'L COUNTERBALANCE THE HEAVY PART OF THE HOOK!

FORCE

FORCE

FULCRUM

THIS IS A CROCK OF BUG DUNG!

It takes a few seconds more to tie a Compara-Dun right but so few commercial tiers will take the time. **Not to worry** .... You can fix these patterns. With your thumb bend the deer hair and crimp it so that it stands up at 90 degrees to the body. Make sure it's spread out in a 180-degree fan when viewed head on.

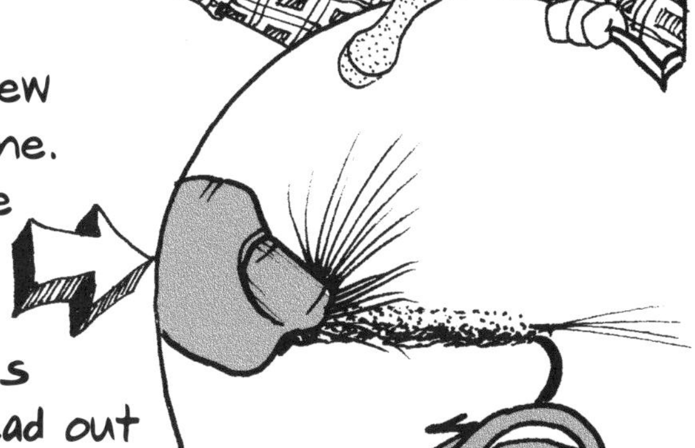

On the water I fish, I've found the dun hatch is much preferred over the spinner hatch. The ability to use the same fly for both hatches makes this fact irrelevant. When the trout are taking spinners the take is usually more relaxed, kind of in a slurping manner.

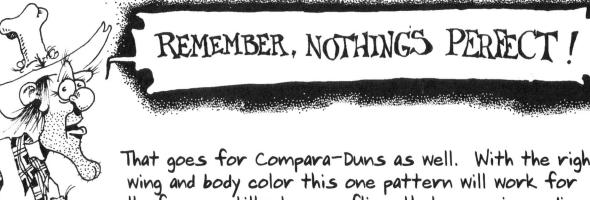

REMEMBER, NOTHING'S PERFECT!

That goes for Compara-Duns as well. With the right wing and body color this one pattern will work for all of your stillwater mayflies that come in medium sizes. However, Compara-Duns do not tie well in sizes below size 18, nor will they float hooks well in patterns above size 10.

SO MUCH FOR THE GOOD ... NOW LET'S LOOK AT THE BAD AND THE UGLY!

THE BAD

The old-timers called the Trico hatch the "fisherman's curse." Like a bad spirit, the Trico hatch was the one insect these guys dreaded.

Tricos are not feared like they once were, in part because manufacturers now are able to produce smaller hooks and finer tying threads resulting in the ability to tie smaller flies.

Actual Size...

...An' this's a big one!

Tricos are found in streams, and chances are you are already familiar with them. Their stillwater counterpart, the little white-winged sulphurs, are the stillwater counterpart to the "curse." For years I assumed they were from the same family but in fact the little sulphurs are Caenidae, or Caenis for short. This aside, when the fish key in on these tiny puppies it can be all they will take, and if you don't have the right fly you too will feel cursed.

Unlike the *Callibaetis*, in which the fish prefer the duns, the little white-winged sulphur's dun phase is not as important as the spinner stage. I don't know why the fish prefer duns of one species and spinners of another, but they do.

Pre-bifocal White-Winged Sulphur

(size 18–22)

seen from above

Post-bifocal White-Winged Sulphur

(size 16 or 14)

Just like Tricos, your little sulphurs will cluster during the spinner fall. I don't know who first thought of tying cluster flies but it is a pretty clever idea. The larger hook makes finding the eye of the hook a whole lot easier.

107

It doesn't matter which of these two patterns you use or how good your eyes are, if you look away you can have a hard time finding your fly again.

A long cast under low-light conditions can sometimes mean you can't find your fly to start with. You can correct this by;

raising your rod...

...until your fly leaves a little wake.

This will allow you to find your fly again.

Sometimes lighting and water conditions (such as small waves) will still make finding your fly hard or impossible. This is where you have to use the old "horse shoes and hand grenade" approach....another one of the few times when closeness counts. Make your best guess as to the approximate position of your fly and draw a mental image of the area around your fly. If you see any rise in that area set the hook. It should be obvious that the smaller your target area the better your odds are when the conditions force you to use this technique.

strike zone

The new tying materials and better hooks have taken a lot of the curse out of these small flies. My choice as the curse for the next millennium is *Daphnia,* but more on that later.

108

The last mayfly in our good, bad, and ugly series shouldn't be thought of as ugly but rather BIG and ugly.

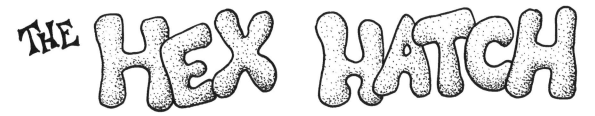

THE HEX HATCH

The lack of beauty in the Hex nymph is rivaled only by the dinosaur-like appearance of a large stonefly nymph. The first adult I ever saw fly by I mistook for a slow-flying hummingbird. The nymph and the adult are both colossal.

Hex nymph   Hex dun

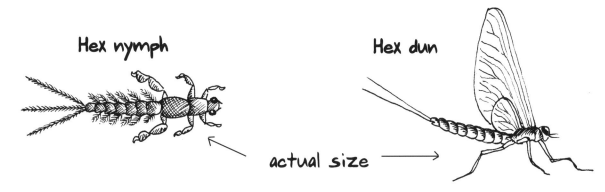

actual size ⟶

Hex's nickname comes from its Latin name *Hexagenia limbata*. Because its size makes it so obvious, early fishermen recognized its importance right off and gave it a bunch of common names. Depending on where you fish, it is called a fish fly, sand fly, or Michigan caddis. Michigan caddis is confusing because it is not a caddis but a mayfly. If you come across this reference in an old book you won't be fooled.

IT'S ABOUT TIME WE TALK ABOUT A REAL MEAL AND NOT AN HORS D'OEUVRE!

Hex is one of the few species that is found in both rivers and lakes. The type of water is less important than the type of bottom. As the Hex nymph is a burrower it needs just the right kind of bottom material to build its home, which is a "U"-shaped affair with an entrance and an exit. Here the nymph can come out at night and feed. During the day it hides and does whatever nymphs do during the day.

Tunnel is about five inches deep.

After spending one or two years in the tunnel the nymph is ready to emerge. The emergence will happen when the weather is pretty warm. Look for these guys from mid-summer through early fall.

The duns like to start off the water the last half hour of light. They keep emerging until total darkness.

I've watched the duns emerge and they are only on the surface for a couple of seconds before they fly off. Typical of all insects that make a quick escape, the duns are hit fast and hard by the trout.

Hint #1: Very few will come off during the day. If you see this, then make sure you come back just before dark.

Hint #2: Hex hatches will last a long time during the summer. Some nights will be better than others, with hatches not very good if a cold front moves in. If you find them on your lake you can expect to see them for a long time.

The dun is usually dirty yellow in color with wings from a dun to brownish yellow in color. There are special problems in fishing large flies with large hooks, such as how to float that much iron on the surface. There are a few realistic patterns, including the Big Yellow May.

Big Yellow May

This is one big fly !

Like a handle on a tool, the shank of a hook will produce more leverage the longer it is. After a couple of fish, flies just don't float as well. When the Big Yellow May starts to waterlog, the leverage it puts on the hackle will cause it to go down at the stern.

On traditional flies, the longer the shank...

...the easier it will waterlog and sink.

The worse the lighting conditions the less exact the imitation has to be. This is an important lesson for all stillwater fishermen. I have found that a good imitation for the Hex hatch in the evening is Kaufmann's Yellow Stimulator. Although this fly was developed as a golden stone pattern for rivers, the hackled body supports a large hook well, and the trout take it with gusto.

The spinner fall for the Hex happens from midnight on. To tell you the truth, I've never stayed up to learn how to fish it. I mention it only because there are still a few mysteries that have not been covered yet in all the magazines. For this you are on your own. Be aware: Not all states allow fishing after dark.

The Carey Special

Like most nymphs that burrow, they are accessible only when they come out at night to feed. I have had good success with a Carey Special fished on the bottom. As best as I can determine by looking down in the water, the Hex nymphs prefer a kind of sandy bottom. I think it is best for tunnel building. Now, it is possible that the fish are hitting the Carey not as a Hex pattern, but as a leech or dragonfly. It's one of those things that works that I can't explain.

Fact: No other hatches are kept as secret as the Hex hatches. You have to be a real Sherlock Holmes to pry the information out of fellow fly fishermen. Even some of the guys in the fly shops are tight-lipped about Hex hatches.

Few snags on a sandy bottom

Hint: Keep you ears peeled for reports of guys who see the shucks from stoneflies floating on the lake. Since there are no stoneflies it means......
Hex is here !

OK! NOW YOU HAVE SEEN THE MAMA BEAR, PAPA BEAR, AND BABY BEAR OF MAYFLIES...

...which gives you some considerations for fishing small, medium, and large mayflies.

You might find different hatches, especially for the medium-sized mayflies like the *Callibaetis* that we covered here, but all things considered, they are fished the same way, just with different flies. If you remember one thing, it should be to match your fly to the color of the mayfly's belly. Also, you match the size of your fly to the hatch, you can't go wrong.

Hint: As they come off the water, all species of mayflies will have wings that are the same shape. As they hold their wings together over their backs they give one the impression of a small sailboat. Remember this and you will never confuse the mayflies with any other order of insects.

Both a sail....
and a wing are shaped and positioned the same way.

Since a mayfly can't tack, look for them on the downwind shore.

the CADDISFLY

Caddisflies are far and away the most interesting of the aquatic insects. Not only do they build their own houses but some of the river caddis make life lines, much like a mountain climber, so that they don't get swept away in the current. Other river caddisflies build nets to catch food. Unfortunately the lake caddis is a little less exciting but is still an important insect for fish.

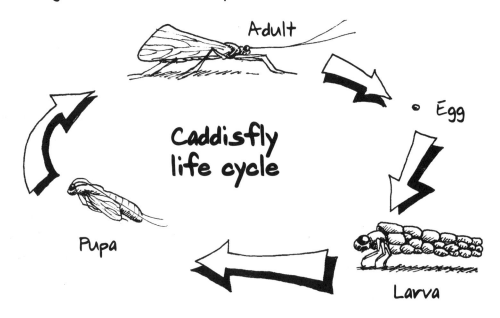

Caddisflies are often confused with stoneflies but there are two features that are unique to caddis that will help with identification.

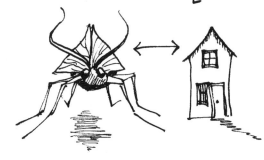

Caddisflies don't have tails; stoneflies do. Even easier, all caddisflies have wings that look like a roof, while stonefly wings lay down flat on their back. This is a dead giveaway and foolproof for identification.

Most stillwater caddis imitations target the pupa and the adult. The larva is usually on the bottom and moves so slowly that most imitations will get snagged on the bottom.

When caddisflies get within a couple of weeks of emerging the larva seals itself in and transforms into a pupa. This is just like what a butterfly or moth does...only it happens underwater. A half an hour or so before the hatch starts it works open its case and with the aid of an inflatable air bag around its body, floats to the surface. Most caddisflies then inflate their wings and, in a matter of seconds, fly away.

Some caddis, when they come back to lay their eggs, will land on the water or dip along close to the surface to lay their eggs. Some will land on reeds along the shore and climb down the reeds until they are under water and then lay their eggs.

Fishin' The Caddis

Unlike mayflies or damsels, the pupa of the caddisfly is not found swimming around all the time. It is important to remember that these little guys are found only half an hour or so before the hatch begins.

Never pick these flies to explore the water as a searching pattern when you can't determine where or on what the fish are feeding.

Often the first indication that a caddis hatch is happening is when you see the adults taking off. This means you have missed the opportunity to fish the pupa. Most of us would prefer to fish a dry fly when we can to watch the strike. However, take note of the time and on your next visit start fishing the pupa about forty-five minutes before the hatch is due to happen.

FISH PUPAE ON a LONG LEADER OVER PLAECS WHERE YOU SEE ADULT CADDIS RISING

long leader

...like most other bugs, the caddis will have a favorite area of the lake.

Hint: The ascent is slow so your retrieve should reflect this.

Hint: Use your stomach pump to determine size and color of the pupa the fish are feeding on.

There are a lot of realistic fly patterns for fishing the pupa. Give some of these a try. Simplicity has always worked for me; a simple fly that is easy to tie is the old and unglamorous Soft Hackle. It has the added advantage of imitating a drowned midge or mayfly.

Notice the hackle folds back, making it look like a pupa.

This is how it looks dry...

...and this is how it looks wet

Like mayflies, caddis come in all sizes. In frog water there are a lot more micro caddis. These are the little guys size 18 and smaller. Unless you tie your own it is hard to find flies for these caddisflies. In my waters they are common but don't come off in massive hatches. Usually the first indication is sporadic rises to no obvious hatches. You have to look real close to find them.

CDC Caddis

actual size

Here is your CDC Caddis enlarged a whole bunch of times

The relatively new CDC Caddis patterns are my favorite for this hatch. CDC's can be mistaken for a small midge as well. If you don't know my feelings on dual-purpose flies by now...You gotta go back to the beginning of the book and start all over. (I love 'em)

In my waters, fishing micro caddis is a lot like watching grass grow. Yes, there are a lot of them but not in big enough hatches to drive the fish wild. They come off a few at a time.

To be honest, I prefer to fish a Damsel Nymph but on your water it could well be different. Fish your micro caddis patterns dead still, close to, but not over, rises.

SEDGE IS THE ENGLISH WORD FOR CADDIS !

Fly patterns and caddis species from Canada and England are usually called sedges.

All things being equal, caddisflies seem to prefer running water to stillwater. It would be foolish not to have a bunch of Elk Hair Caddis in your box if you were stream fishing. If you were fishing a lake and left your caddis flies at home by mistake, you probably wouldn't miss them and it usually wouldn't be a disaster.

On occasion, I've been in hatches that would rival the best of the river hatches. The caddis swirled like dust devils landing behind my glasses and in my mouth. But, for the most part, the caddis is secondary to mayflies, damselflies, and midges.

Sooner or later you will find yourself in one of these hatches. They come in two types: one where the fish are actively feeding on emerging caddis with lots of surface activity; and the second type where the caddis appear to be ignored. The second is by far the most common situation, due in part to the fact that caddis seem to leave the water fast and don't like to stand on it.

It does happen, so when you see fish working a caddis hatch:

first lay your fly close to the rise and let it stay still.

If you have matched the color and size the fish will usually take it.

118

Sometimes the trout like a skated fly. To do this:

Raise the rod.

The fly will move towards the tip.

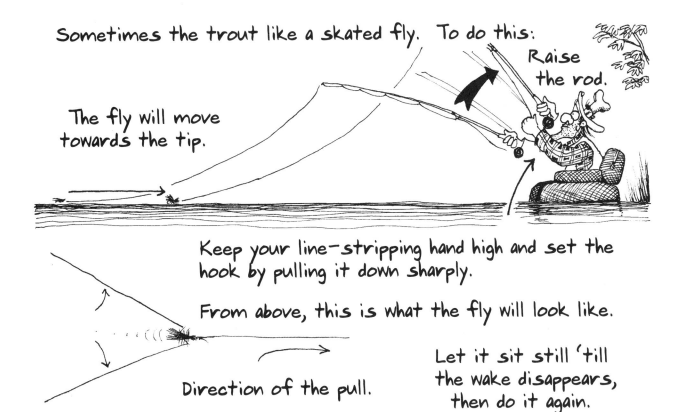

Keep your line-stripping hand high and set the hook by pulling it down sharply.

From above, this is what the fly will look like.

Direction of the pull.

Let it sit still 'till the wake disappears, then do it again.

Elk Hair Caddis flies are real easy to get. Every fly shop carries them but if your fish get a little selective try looking for a Henryville Caddis or one like it, that has a more realistic wing. Of course you have to match the body color to the color of the bugs in your water.

Elk Hair Caddis

Henryville Caddis

Really designed for rivers, this fly will still give good service on most lakes. One big advantage is it floats well and skates even better.

This is a better caddis pattern for duplicating the natural adult. It won't float as well as the Elk Hair, but it fools the fish better.

The most common situation during a caddis hatch is that the adults are ignored. The fish will concentrate on the pupae as they rise to the surface. I figured if Dave Hughes's trick for the *Callibaetis* mayfly worked so well, why not for the caddis as well?

Winged Soft Hackle

I took the same soft-hackle pattern that I used to duplicate the pupa and added a brown turkey wing to look like a caddis wing. I don't know why it works at the height of the hatch but it does. Maybe in large hatches it has a bigger profile which attracts the attention of the fish. It is not available in fly shops, but there are a couple of similar patterns that are. If you want to give it a try, look for these patterns or ones that are similar to these.

Alder fly

Cowdung

Both of these patterns are good for the olive caddis hatches but for cinnamon caddis you are on you own. I suggest buying a vise and a couple of books on fly tying.

When the caddis are swirling and no fish are rising you need to blind cast these patterns, let them settle only a foot or so, and start a slow retrieve. At times it will make you look like a genius.

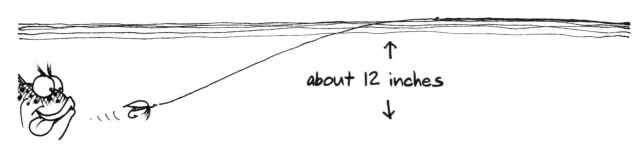

↑

about 12 inches

↓

The Montana stonefly hatch each spring is legendary among fly fishermen. Anglers from all over the world try to hit this hatch and it is truly one of the great moments in a fly-fisher's life. The lake fisherman has a similar hatch, although much less publicized. This is British Columbia's traveling sedge hatch. Like the stonefly hatch, this is one well worth seeing sometime in every fisherman's life.

The traveling sedge hatch is a late-evening, midsummer hatch centered in the Kamloops Lake area of British Columbia. This caddis is found as far south as the northern lakes of Washington State. It is here that I fish them.

The traveling sedge is a fat little puppy that acts like it is too heavy to fly. If its flying skills aren't good, its running skills are superb. Emerging in the middle of a lake at about an-inch-and-a-half long, the caddis starts a sprint for the nearest shore. On calm water he will leave a four-foot-long "V"-wake. The wake and not the pattern seems to be the single factor that fish key in on.

The only way to duplicate the speed of this sprint is with a two-handed retrieve which we will cover a few pages further on. The majority of the trout wait in the area 75 feet from shore and the caddis have to run this blockade. At first I worked my fly so it was always retrieved from the middle towards the shore but soon learned that a parallel cast would put me over more fish.

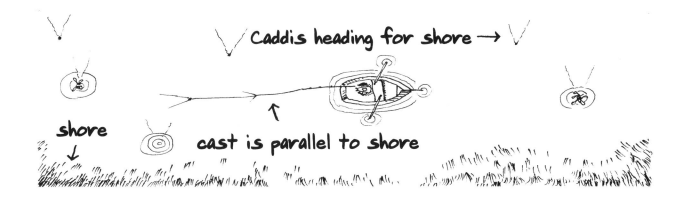

Caddis heading for shore →

cast is parallel to shore

shore

Up in British Columbia, a popular pattern for this hatch is the Tom Thumb, tied totally from deer hair. It doesn't have the right color or the right silhouette...in fact, it is plain "butt ugly." Deer-hair flies ride high in the water and the fish are more attracted by the wake than the pattern so the Tom Thumb works great.

Tom Thumb

The natural has a gray-green body about as big around as a small child's finger. Since the Tom Thumb is rare in most fly boxes, there are a couple of other patterns that will do well should you find yourself in a hatch without a Tom Thumb.

Olive Stimulator

Muddler Minnow

Well-greased, these two flies wake very well. I have used them both with good effect over the traveling Sedge hatch. The trout hit these with real gusto so use a heavy tippet.

ALDERFLIES
(false caddis)

In a lot of areas you can find alderflies that look just like caddis from three feet away. In my water they are all black, wings, body, everything. In some areas they have brown wings and a black body. For right now you have too much entomology to learn, so think of them as black caddis. The real science guys won't be happy but you can get black caddis flies at most fly shops and they are fished the same. We'll get it right later.

Black Caddis

By critical, I mean that you really can't be without those patterns. Almost every lake will have them, and most are there year-round.

It is not so much that the non-critical patterns are not critical, but that they represent special situations. Some of these special situations are **favored by the largest of fish.**

It is real important for an angler to develop a relationship with his water. Learn what is there and even more important when it is there. In this next series of critters fish feed on, you will need to evaluate your water to see if the critters apply to your local conditions. If you are not sure, ask a few questions at your local fly shop.

These guys are found in most waters but only in late summer and early fall. Most fly shops sell *Corixia* named after this insect's family name...Corixidae. Water boatmen, the common name comes from the two long legs that *Corixia* use to row themselves through the water. Fly patterns often bear the common name.

Water boatman

Believe it or not, they are a flying beetle that spends a part of its life in the water. These guys are most common during the late-summer months. This is a time when bugs are getting rare in stillwater. This happens because most of the other insects exist in the egg stage of development at the end of summer. At this time they are waiting to hatch out and winter-over in the nymphal stage.

During this time the waterboatman can play an important role by feeding the fish until the other nymphs hatch out. There are several patterns for this bug but all will look like this.

Corixia
or
Water boatmen

Resting just below the surface film, the waterboatman will dive down at a shallow angle for a few feet then stop and float back to the surface. The floating is accomplished because of the air supply each carries on its stomach. This air bubble will make the natural's stomach look silver.

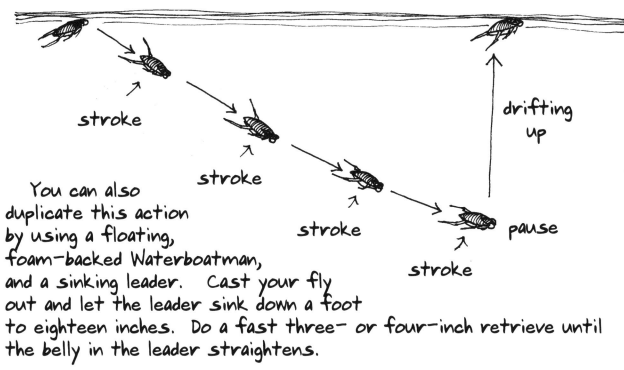

stroke

stroke

stroke

stroke

pause

drifting up

You can also duplicate this action by using a floating, foam-backed Waterboatman, and a sinking leader. Cast your fly out and let the leader sink down a foot to eighteen inches. Do a fast three- or four-inch retrieve until the belly in the leader straightens.

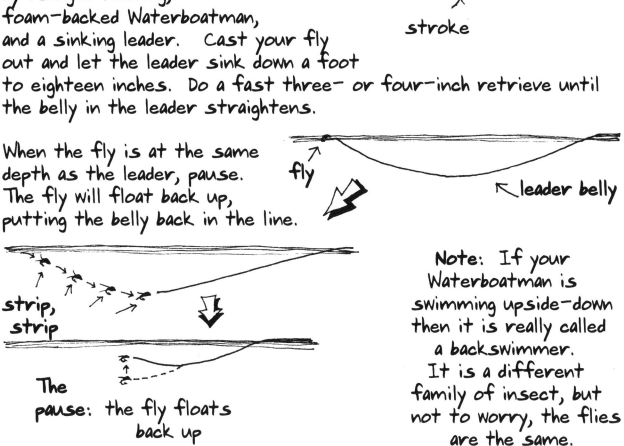

When the fly is at the same depth as the leader, pause. The fly will float back up, putting the belly back in the line.

fly

leader belly

strip, strip

The pause: the fly floats back up

Note: If your Waterboatman is swimming upside-down then it is really called a backswimmer. It is a different family of insect, but not to worry, the flies are the same.

THE "REAL" FISHERMAN'S CURSE
DAPHNIA

A whole lot has been written about the fisheman's curse. Sometimes it is small midges; usually it is small mayflies. In the last twenty years, better and smaller hooks have helped eliminate them as a curse. There is, however, a small critter that can appear from early spring to late fall that deserves the credit for being the curse of the next millenium. This little beast is the *Daphnia* or water flea.

Daphnia
(greatly enlarged)

actual size

These guys are usually red to orange in color. Their populations are sometimes so thick they change the color of the lake. They are too small to make a fly for and the patterns that duplicate mats of *Daphnia* have only met with limited success. I usually wait around for the fish to find another hatch to get them excited. When *Daphnia* are present in great numbers I've learned to expect a slow day. Since they are so small you have to get real close to the water to see them.

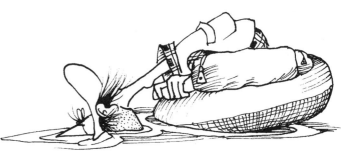

There are fewer terrestrials available to the stillwater fisherman than the stream fisherman. One situation comes to mind that is important and can be fruitful in those lean summer days when action can be slow. The terrestrials I'm referring to are the...

OL' GRASS HOPPERS

On occasion, the wind can pick up, especially on those lakes that occur in open flatlands with little in the way of surrounding tree cover. I'm not talking about a breeze, but a wind that makes you think you ought to go home. This wind can blow hoppers out onto the lake. A quick walk through the grass around the shore will determine if hoppers are present. A real wind will put an end to all other hatches, but not to the need for the fish to eat.

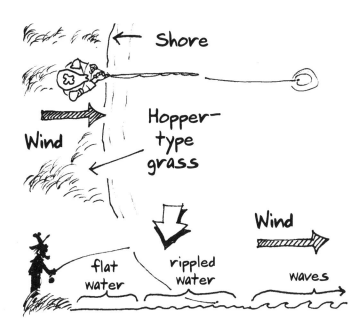

Shore

Wind

Hopper-type grass

Wind

flat water   rippled water   waves

There is a zone on the upwind side of the lake onto which the hoppers will be blown. Plop your fly on the surface and twitch it every minute or so. Even on windy days the thirty feet or so of water on the upwind side will be free of waves. Let the water rings from your twitch disappear for thirty seconds or so before you twitch it again.

Yet another Fish Bum Credo...........................

127

IF YOU ARE GONNA CAST IN THE WIND .... TRY TO ALWAYS CAST DOWNWIND!

...Not only do you reduce the risk of hooking yourself, it is the only way to get any distance at all.

Hopper hint: If you find yourself on a lake when this happens and you don't have a hopper pattern, grease up a Muddler and use it instead. Usually it will work just fine.

Dave's Hopper

Muddler Minnow

As lake-dwelling fish have more time to look over your fly than their river cousins, always pick more natural-looking patterns. Only use the Muddler as a last resort.

Select the color of your flies based on observing the naturals around your lake. They will be yellow, green, or gray and of course you want to match the size as closely as you can.

OK....OK!

So they ain't lobsters, they are really crawdads.   But you gotta admit they sure do look like lobsters, and for big trout, they eat like lobster too.

Just like lobsters, crawdads are bottom-dwellers.   On the bottom they will build a den under a rock or sunken log and come out to forage for food.   When disturbed, they are capable of jetting through the water backwards at considerable speed.   Fishing these patterns can be difficult if you have a weedy bottom or lots of snags.   I like to fish a weighted fly very slowly, in less than ten feet of water, right on the bottom.   If there is a breeze, I wind-drift and every minute or two do a panicked quick strip as if the crawdad was frightened by a fish.

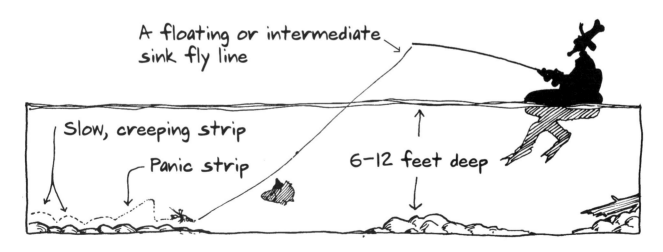

A floating or intermediate sink fly line

Slow, creeping strip

Panic strip

6-12 feet deep

129

Like the naturals, crawdad flies come in a lot of different colors. Black, orange, brown and olive are the most common colors. Check your local lakes and ask questions to find which colors are best suited for your conditions.

All flies that fish on the bottom present special problems. A weighted fly only makes most of these problems worse. Snagging and fouling are the two biggest problems. When you select your patterns try and find a crawdad pattern that will ride hook-up. The hook-down patterns are more for river fishing where a swimming crawdad can be swept downstream by a strong current. These flies will cause aggravation to no end if your lake bottom likes to grab flies.

Keep in mind that not all lakes are suitable for fishing these patterns. The payoff is that you won't catch little fish. These are food for the big guys. There is always a tradeoff, nothing is perfect.

Pick patterns with their hook up,
like this.

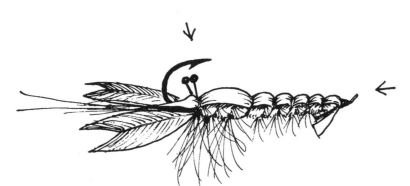

Crawfish

Note:
The down-turned eye is up when the hook is upside-down. This helps make it act like a jig hook.

I bet ninety percent of even the good fishermen don't use these patterns. This is not an easy fly to tie or to fish, but for those who are willing to go the extra mile, this fly can pay off big time.

RODENTS

All kinds of little rodent-type critters live along the shores of lakes. It was only a decade ago that I was introduced to night fishing the mouse pattern. To be honest with you I don't know if mice like to go skinny dipping under the moonlight or not. What I do know is that this technique will work, especially if you have a population of brown trout.

Cast your fly up on the shore and let it set there until everything goes quiet. Then pull your fly onto the water and slowly swim it back to the rod. I do this mostly on desert lakes as the water near home is too brushy. It can be pretty exciting!

fly on the shore

retrieve just fast enough to leave a wake

You will pick up bass if they are present, but brown trout love this, especially the big ones.

Alaska fishermen have long-used lemming patterns for large rainbows in their rivers. Some will tell you when picking out a fly make sure it has whiskers. There is a belief that this is important to the fish.

The Deer Hair Mouse

Your basic mouse pattern is mostly a bass pattern and may come with a weed guard. I like to cut it off.

Tail: important

Ears: not important

Whiskers: maybe important

As a fine example of how much of our fishing is done by current fashion and not logic, take a look at baitfish. Baitfish and the streamers that imitate them are hardly ever mentioned in respect to both river and stillwater trout fishing. The one exception is sculpin patterns. Baitfish are a very productive and important category overlooked by too many fishermen.

Remember: Trout over 18 inches will feed readily on small fish, and will cannibalize their own!

IF ONLY WE COULD GET THE JET SKIERS TO DO THAT!

HE HE

Almost every lake will have a breeding population of some sort of fish. Sculpins or bullheads are, of course, the most popular, but sticklebacks, shad, dace, bluegill, perch, crappie, and largemouth will produce young. And don't forget the cannibalistic characteristic of the trout themselves. I once caught a brown trout that threw up five largemouth bass in the net. The thing to remember is that you want to fish patterns that

132

imitate the species in your water before they grow more than three or so inches long. Often, like a good hatch, the opportunity to fish these patterns comes shortly after they hatch out. At this time they are quite small. Ideally an inch or two is the perfect size. You will want to do some research on your waters to find out what species might lend themselves to duplicating with streamers.

As a fly tier I make a generic streamer that does pretty well in imitating a wide range of small fish species. You may find something similar in the saltwater fly selection of your local fly shop. I divide the fish into two categories—deep-bodied minnows and slender-bodied minnows—and tie my flies accordingly.

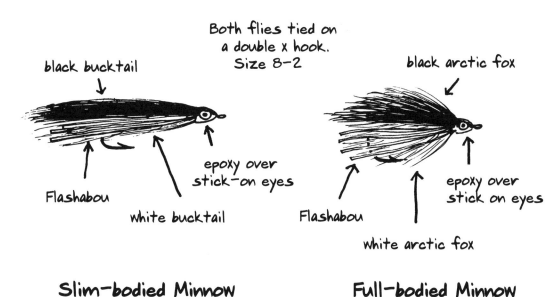

black bucktail

Both flies tied on a double x hook.
Size 8-2

black arctic fox

Flashabou

epoxy over stick-on eyes

white bucktail

Flashabou

epoxy over stick on eyes

white arctic fox

Slim-bodied Minnow   **Full-bodied Minnow**

A majority of the small minnows you see along the shore appear to have a black back. These two flies will do well as a starting point for small baitfish. If you have yellow perch or bass you will want to look for patterns that better represent these fish.

Most small fish frequent the shallows for protection. You often find them in small bays. They are also found around structure like sunken logs and brush, as well as along the weed beds. Small islands and shoals are some of my favorite places.

I like to use my floating lines to hit these shallow places.

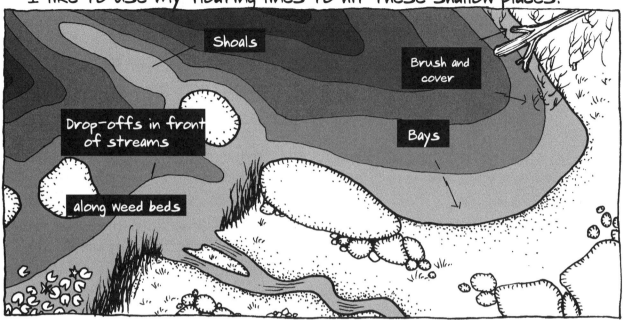

When fishing streamers you want your retrieve to represent a panicked or wounded minnow. A fast and erratic retrieve will often tempt a large trout looking for a meal of opportunity.

The most popular and well-known minnows belong to the sculpin family. These little fellows are found almost everywhere. They have become a favorite fly among knowledgeable fishermen. Unlike spiny ray fish, most sculpins have no real spine to make swallowing them difficult. As a result they depend on stealth and coloration for survival. Most will sit quietly on the bottom and wait for their own meal, moving only to feed or when frightened.

The first sculpin pattern was the Muddler Minnow, but in recent years the Woolhead Sculpin has come on the scene. I much prefer the Woolhead to the Muddler because the wool is easier to dye and tie, and therefore produces a fly that can more closely duplicate the color and shape of the natural.

Muddler Minnow

Woolhead Sculpin

I fish the sculpin in the same waters that I fish the other minnow patterns except I use a sink-tip or full-sinking line. Remember these guys are bottom-dwellers and, as such, should be fished close to where the fish is used to seeing them. If you have sculpins in your water, these flies are an absolute must for larger fish.

With so much regional variation I don't want to give advice on this category. Start by asking at your fly shop, but you're on your own.

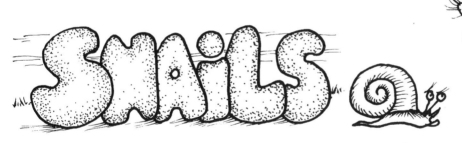

HEY! WHAT DO YOU EXPECT? AFTER ALL ... THIS AIN'T A FORTY DOLLAR BOOK!

Snails have the ability to change depth by filling themselves with air. Midsummer trout can feed heavily on these guys. You can tell when you release a fish as you will feel hard, rock-like things in its stomach. Fish your patterns very slowly from a strike indicator or on the surface. I usually fish the top 18 inches of water.

Moose Mane Snail

Chenille Snail

HOW MANY FLIES ARE YOU GONNA NEED?

Let's take a look at how many flies you need for a two-day trip, to a local lake. As an example, let's look at the best of the spring flies, the Chironomid. Let's start with a size 14 as this is the median size, and add flies larger and smaller of less importance. On a normal day we will need two flies to leave in the weeds or in brush along the shore, two to leave in large fish, and two to give to our fishing partner. Remember Croft's Law:

CROFT'S LAW: THE FISH WILL ONLY HIT PATTERNS NOT FOUND IN YOUR PARTNER'S FLY BOX!

True!

This means, that to ensure you will have enough flies to get through a day you need to have six flies of a pattern, in a particular color and size.

But since we are fishing for two days... we need about 12.

But this is only one size! Let's say we want to have samples of the other sizes and keep the numbers proportionate to their relative importance.

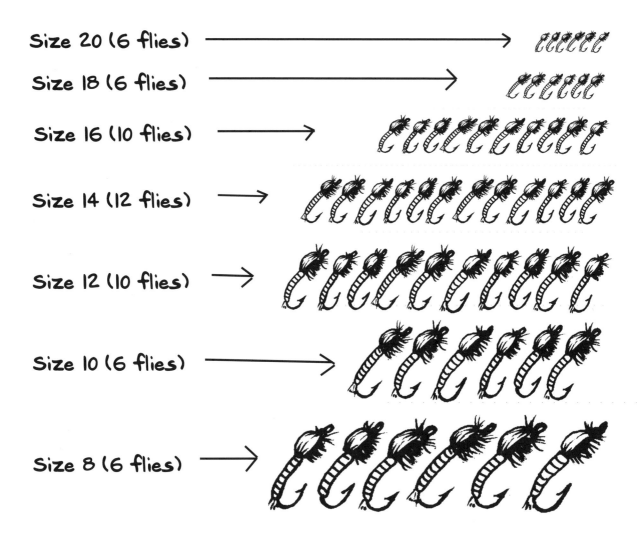

Size 20 (6 flies)

Size 18 (6 flies)

Size 16 (10 flies)

Size 14 (12 flies)

Size 12 (10 flies)

Size 10 (6 flies)

Size 8 (6 flies)

Note: Your mean average size will be different depending on how far north you live, with larger chironomids appearing north and smaller in the south. But it won't effect the numbers much.

Now this is only one color, let's say it's black. What if they are hitting olive instead? Or how about tan? Maybe red! My personal Chironomid box has black, tan, brown, light olive, dark olive, and red. It also contains some special chironomids with things like moose-mane bodies. Turn the page to see what a proper box looks like.

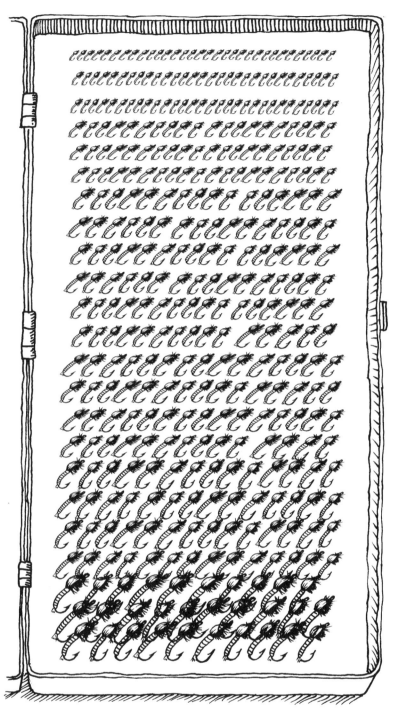

For seven colors it totals up to 382 flies.

What this gives you is a box that will be able to handle 99% of all the midge pupa situations that you encounter on the water.

The down side is that a box like this is worth about $500, or at least that is about what it would cost you to fill it at most fly shops.

This exercise needs to be done in each color and size for each species in the first section on entomology.

Remember that you won't need each size and color on every trip, but this is the ideal box for all conditions. At the end of the weekend you need only replace what you lost or loaned out.

If you haven't guessed it by now, I see a fly-tying class in your future. After all, that is why they invented closed seasons. It gives a fly tier time to refill his boxes. But, more on the art of fly tying a little later on.

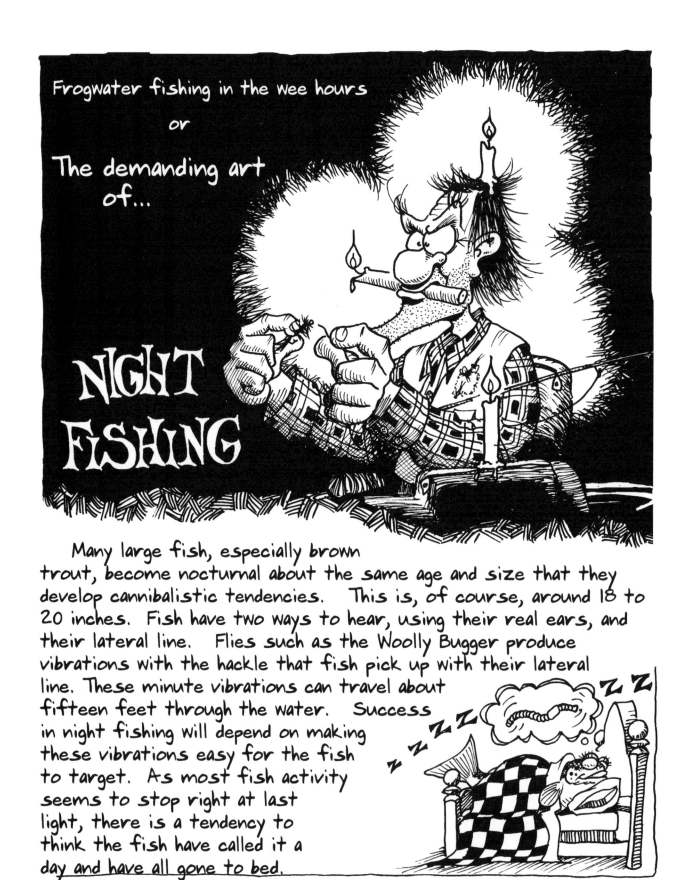

Frogwater fishing in the wee hours

or

The demanding art of...

NIGHT FISHING

Many large fish, especially brown trout, become nocturnal about the same age and size that they develop cannibalistic tendencies. This is, of course, around 18 to 20 inches. Fish have two ways to hear, using their real ears, and their lateral line. Flies such as the Woolly Bugger produce vibrations with the hackle that fish pick up with their lateral line. These minute vibrations can travel about fifteen feet through the water. Success in night fishing will depend on making these vibrations easy for the fish to target. As most fish activity seems to stop right at last light, there is a tendency to think the fish have called it a day and have all gone to bed.

This is _not_ the case. A fish's pupil doesn't work like ours. To control the amount of light on their retinas, fish have to change the shape of their eyes. This little effort can take up to an hour. This is why fish often seem to go off the bite. An hour after dark is when the bite usually starts up, although my favorite time is from midnight to about 3:00 a.m.

You want to use flies that have a lot of hackle or deer hair so that you can produce as many underwater vibrations as possible. Your strip should be evenly spaced so that the fish can hear and anticipate where your fly will be when it decides to hit it. Imagine every pull as a flash from a lighthouse. Keep them regular!

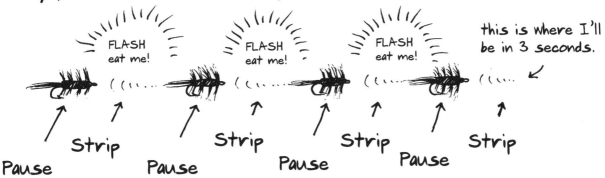

Casting is not easy in the dark so keep your casts short. It is much easier to paddle around in a float tube or small boat giving a small strip to your line every three or four seconds.

A TANGLE IN THE DARK EQUALS TEN IN THE LIGHT!

In the wee hours a tangle is your worst enemy. Go slow and deliberate to help prevent this.

Distance is real hard to judge in the dark, so fishing the shallows is hard if there is a lot of weeds and bulrushes present. To avoid these potential tangle problems concentrate on drop-offs, shoals, and points where the water is shallow but open.

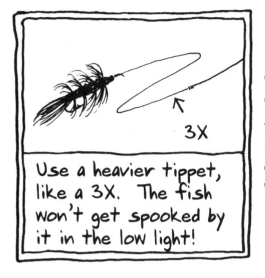

Use a heavier tippet, like a 3X. The fish won't get spooked by it in the low light!

For casting in the dark, a soft-action fly rod is ideal. Distance is not as important as it is when you are sight-fishing during daylight. A soft rod will flex clear to the butt and this added tactile input is real nice when you can't see your fly line.

Another reson to use a heavier tippet when night fishing is that the fish have a tendancy to really pound your fly. There are no gentle takes, and the biggest fish are active at this time. The darker it is, the better they seem to hit. This means fish the dark of the moon.

soft rod
flexes clear to herel

I use two patterns for night fishing: a Woolly Bugger and the mouse pattern we talked about earlier. The mouse pattern is natural deer hair so its color is gray. The Woolly Buggers I use are usually black. One would think that a black fly at night doesn't make much sense, but if the stars are out it will block out the starlight as it passes over a fish. Remember, too, the primary sensory organ is going to be the lateral line, making color less important. When selecting flies for night fishing look for the Woolly Buggers with the stiffest hackles. These are the ones that will do the most vibrating.

Nuts to...

KNOTS

HOW MANY TIMES...

...HAVE YOU BUSTED OFF A FISH AND THE TIPPET LOOKED LIKE THIS?

Tippet
30X
magnification

Is your knot of choice the cinch or fisherman's knot? You know, the one that looks like this....

...then you may be a victim of tradition!
If you answered yes to both of the above questions then you have probably experienced "knot slip."

  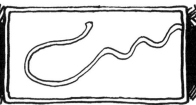

This is a real break..   ...and so is this...   ...This is a knot that has slipped!

More fish are lost to this knot slipping than are broken off. It is the absolute worst knot you can use. The only good thing about this knot is that it is easy to tie.

THE FREEDOM ···er··· FISHERMAN'S KNOT IS A FINE KNOT··· KEEP USING IT! HE HE.

There is a knot you can tie in less than ten seconds. A knot that never slips, a knot you can tie in total darkness....after you get the tippet through the eye. The only place you will find this knot is in Darrel Martin's book *Fly-Tying Methods*, where he calls it the weaver's knot.

The Weaver's Knot

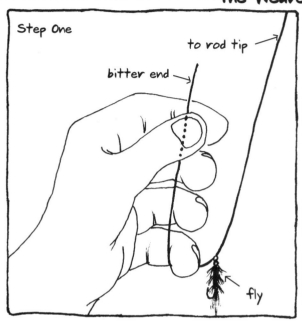

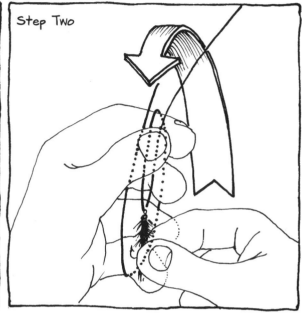

Step one: Thread tippet through the eye, and hold bitter end with palm of the left hand facing you.

Step two: Pull the fly over the back of your left hand and grasp the loop with your left hand thumb.

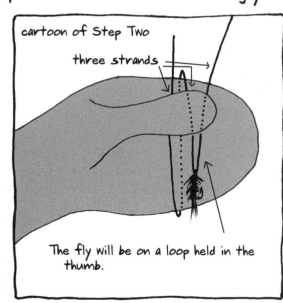

The fly will be on a loop held in the thumb.

No, No, NO! You don't have to slip on a mitten! I just wanted to draw the point at which we should be after Step Two, without any confusing lines for fingers and such.

You should have the illusion that your thumb is holding three strands of line. The fly should be hanging from a loop, below the thumb.

144

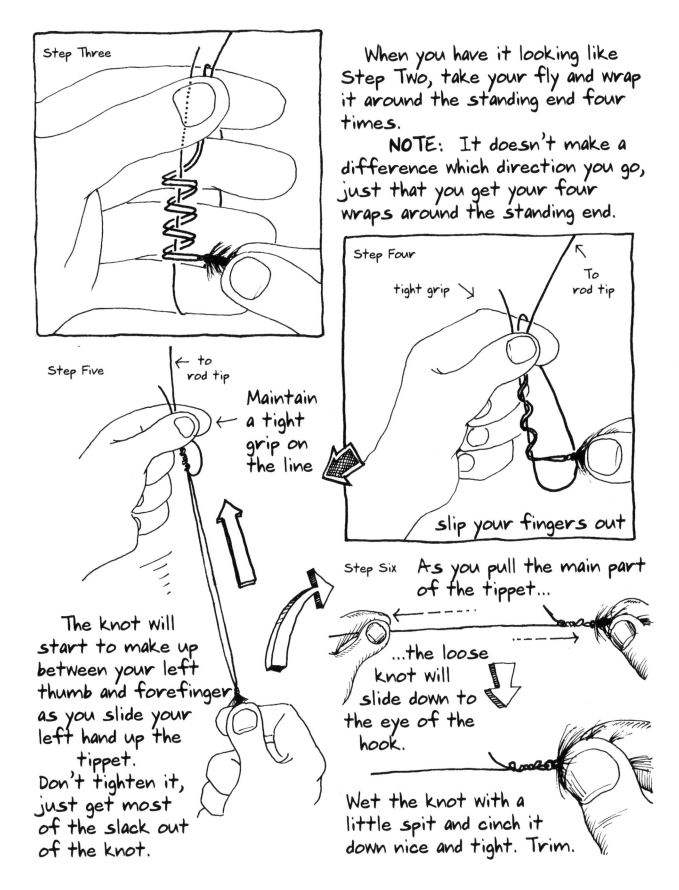

Step Three

When you have it looking like Step Two, take your fly and wrap it around the standing end four times.

NOTE: It doesn't make a difference which direction you go, just that you get your four wraps around the standing end.

Step Four

tight grip ↘

To rod tip ↖

slip your fingers out

Step Five

← to rod tip

Maintain a tight grip on the line

The knot will start to make up between your left thumb and forefinger as you slide your left hand up the tippet.
Don't tighten it, just get most of the slack out of the knot.

Step Six As you pull the main part of the tippet...

...the loose knot will slide down to the eye of the hook.

Wet the knot with a little spit and cinch it down nice and tight. Trim.

The weaver knot has the advantage of not tightening until it makes contact with the eye of the hook. The fisherman's knot on the other hand tightens before it slides down to the eye of the hook. This stretches the tippet material and gives the last couple of inches in front of the eye a characteristic pig tail curl.

The weaver's knot

The fisherman's knot

see how the tippet is nice and straight

pig tail-shaped friction curl from...

...quickly tied knot

When fishing Chironomids, the take is gentle and the rejection is very fast. The fly is spit out the second the fish realizes it is not real food. The straighter the contact to the fly the faster information is transmitted to the angler. A pig tail takes a little time to straighten out. This is not a problem with the weaver knot.

"LIL" TRIVIA

CAN FISH TASTE ?

You bet they do! That is why there are no fly patterns...

...for water skippers or water striders. These guys produce a foul chemical that makes them taste bad.

Is it possible that one insect could taste better than another?

WATER STRIDER

WOULD YOU CHOOSE A SODA CRACKER OVER A GLAZED DONUT ?

Fetching back your fly
or
THE ART OF THE...

RETRIEVE

In stillwater, your retrieve is more important than on rivers or creeks because there is no current to give life to your fly. There is no letting your fly swing down and across, anything your fly does other than sink you gotta do yourself. The real key to successful retrieves is to observe the naturals.

Retrieves fall under a couple of categories. There are a few things you can do to aid in your success. The most important thing to do, whatever retrieve you use, is...

NEVER LOSE CONTACT WITH YOUR FLY !!!

Always have your fly line anchored with one or the other of your hands. If you are doing a simple strip retrieve and holding the rod in your right hand while reaching up to get another grip on the fly line with your left hand, don't let the line rest on your index finger ANCHOR IT WITH YOUR INDEX FINGER!

Imagine your left hand is reaching up to grab your line for the next strip. Never let your index finger stay open during the reach. Anchor it like in the drawing on the right.

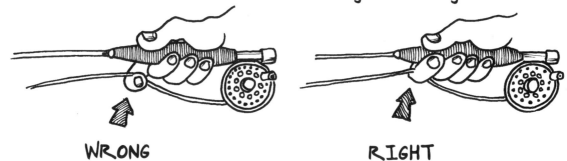

WRONG   RIGHT

It is a little clumsy at first because you need to let go with the anchoring finger to make the next strip. Most of you have experienced grabbing the fly line only to feel it going out. Before you can set the hook the fish has already spit out the fly. Anchoring your line will prevent most of this from happening and your percentage of hookups will increase.

The incident that caused the fish to hit is brought on by the most important part of the retrieve......the PAUSE!

THAT'S RIGHT! YOUR BEST RETRIEVE IS NO RETRIEVE AT ALL!

Everything that swims will pause. Learn to copy the pause or resting period of the natural. Learn how long a damsel nymph stops to get its breath. Learn the pause of the Chironomid pupa and the resting period of the leech, then do them in your retrieve. The fish will respond to these presentations.

A FULL TWO-THIRDS OF YOUR FISH WILL HIT DURING THE PAUSE!

Don't think you can just "plunk" your fly. Fish seem to hit the fly during the pause as a way of recognizing the fly's vulnerability. You will be a better fisherman if you master the pause, especially when fishing nymphs and subsurface flies.

Have you heard this?

NANA... YOU FLY FISHERMEN CAN'T DO A CONTINUOUS RETRIEVE LIKE US SPIN FISHERMEN!

Well, there are two ways to do a continous retrieve and I'm going to show you the easiest. It might sound like a contradiction to talk about a continuous retrieve right after I pushed "the pause," but you should use them together. The naturals move fast and the continuous retrieve allows you to fish baitfish and streamer patterns quickly to match this movement.

149

After you cast, stick your rod under your arm...

LIKE THIS!

then...

Strip in your line hand-over-hand like pulling in an anchor rope.

This is an old-time favorite of saltwater fishermen. You don't set the hook with your armpit but with a quick jerk of your hand. You do have to get your rod clear of your armpit before the fish takes out all the slack line. Do this and your reel won't foul in your vest.

You can control the speed from real slow to rocket fast. I use this retrieve mostly for streamers but have had good success at times with Woolly Buggers and even scuds. Don't forget to throw in a pause or two to let following fish catch up.

Watching paint dry....or the

CHIRONOMID RETRIEVE

Usually you are retrieving a strike indicator a foot or two above your Chironomid pupa. To do this properly use very small strips- about an inch per strip-and do them slowly. A lot of anglers feel this is too boring to do and prefer to fish other flies. Too bad for them!

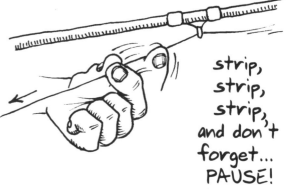

strip, strip, strip, and don't forget... PAUSE!

the HAND WEAVE

When I was learning this retrieve, after an hour or so I started getting hand cramps. This one doesn't come naturally but is very good at imitating the slow and deliberate swimming action of the subsurface nymph.

Start by grabbing your fly line with the thumb and fore finger of your left hand. The rod is in your right hand (reverse if you're left-handed).

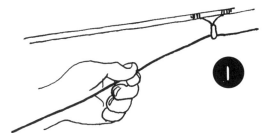

Rotate your hand back towards you (see arrow) while reaching over the line with your other three fingers. You will have brought in about four inches of line.

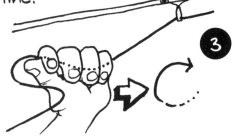

Grasp the line in your hand and rotate your wrist forward again (see arrow). Another four inches of line will come in.

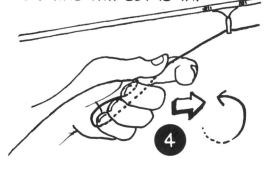

Like Step One, grab the line with your forefinger and rotate the wrist again. Now you have 12 inches of line in your palm.

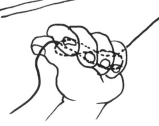

Keep doing this until your hand fills with line. When your hand is full just drop it and keep going until the fly is back, or you get either a fish or a cramp.

No matter which retrieve you use, remember...

NEVER...

...RETRIEVE WITH YOUR ROD UP IN THE AIR LIKE THIS!

You won't have enough rod room to set the hook. Keep your rod tip close to the water!

Hint: If your retrieve isn't working–I mean you aren't catching fish–then change it, speed it up or slow it down. Experiment until you find a combination that works. It will change from day to day, every day.

Now, I'm going to get teased about this but one of the most important things you can do to improve your retrieve is gonna sound a lot like Zen. Try to "be" the bug. I mean, use your imagination and pretend you are your fly. Forget the scenery and the lake and everything around you and concentrate on what it is like to swim back to your rod.

If you do this your hand will pause when you think your insect should rest. You will also find that you will slow your retrieve down to a pace that will represent what the naturals do. Except for concentrating, it is effortless, what's more, it works. You will have to check back to reality every so often to make sure you are not missing a hatch or some such thing.

HE HE

READING THE WATER

Most fish like structure. They like points, shoals, weed beds, and drop offs. The best way to find this structure is to find a contour map of the lake bottom. Often you don't have the time or you fish a lake out of impulse instead of approaching it like a military campaign. Without a map you have to use your intuitive reasoning.

Usually, what happens above water will extend out into the lake.

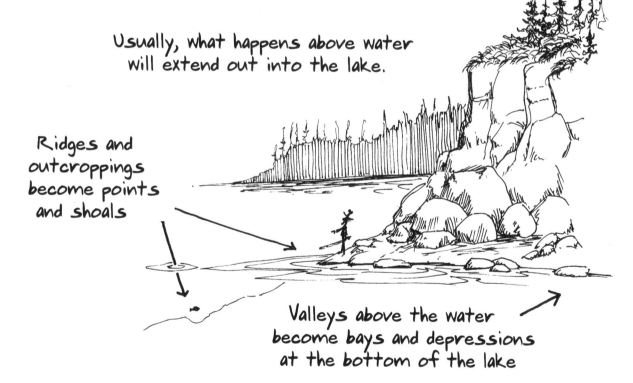

Ridges and outcroppings become points and shoals

Valleys above the water become bays and depressions at the bottom of the lake

This is a rough estimation, and doesn't replace a good map, but it will help you determine where to start on a new and unknown body of water.

153

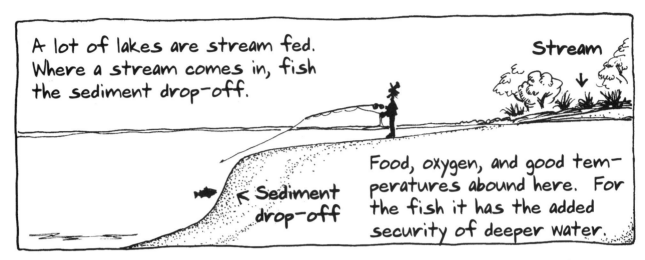

A lot of lakes are stream fed. Where a stream comes in, fish the sediment drop-off.

Stream

← Sediment drop-off

Food, oxygen, and good temperatures abound here. For the fish it has the added security of deeper water.

All lakes have some gradient to the bottom. Try, as much as possible, to always fish up the gradient. Most of the fish, when not feeding on a surface hatch, will be found within a foot or two of the bottom. Fishing up the sloop will keep your fly in their face a lot longer, and over a greater distance on the bottom.

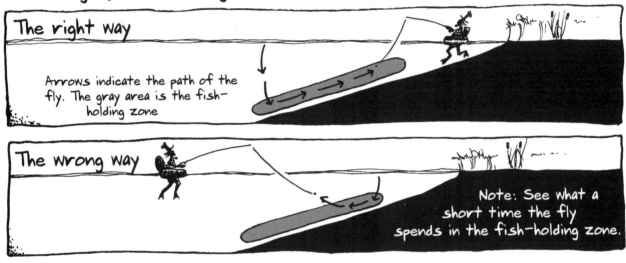

The right way

Arrows indicate the path of the fly. The gray area is the fish-holding zone

The wrong way

Note: See what a short time the fly spends in the fish-holding zone.

Maybe you shouldn't think of it as a wrong or a right way but as two different ways. It is not always possible to fish "the right way" as you can frighten some fish in shallow water. While "the wrong way" may spend little time in the usual fish-holding zone, it does allow you to fish a wider variety of depths. This means you can hit fish during those times when they are moving between the bottom and the surface. Eighty percent of the time you want to try and retrieve your fly up the sloop if this position is possible.

Don't think that because lakes are termed "stillwater" that there are no currents. I would guess that the majority of a lake's currents are generated by the wind. As long as it's not too windy to fish, take a close look at points that are perpendicular to the direction of the wind.

All the critters that get blown onto the upwind side of the point will eventually wash down and around the point, with a heavy concentration of them along the seam.

The Wind Slick: A moderate wind phenomenon.

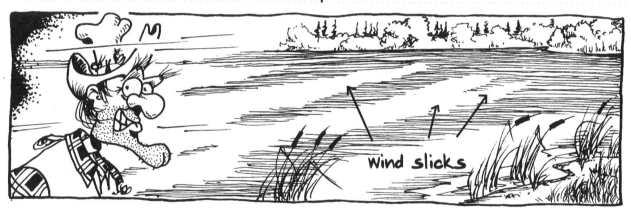

In light to moderate wind conditions you will find wind slicks forming on your lake. Fish cruising the deeper parts of the lake will often rise right along the edges of these slicks. I think they like the edges because the rippled water protects them from air attacks by birds. The slick water makes finding the surface insects easier for the fish. The best of both worlds for the fish is right along the edge where they can feed and hide at the same time. In heavy winds the slicks disappear and the whole lake will turn to white caps. In "no-wind" conditions the fish go deeper.

Wind will cause a current above the thermocline that will change the type of fishing from one side of the lake to the other.

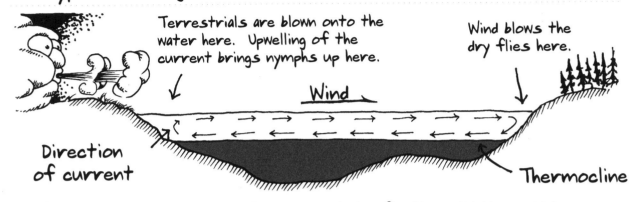

Terrestrials are blown onto the water here. Upwelling of the current brings nymphs up here.

Wind blows the dry flies here.

Wind

Direction of current

Thermocline

Of course leeches, nymphs, and a lot of other little critters aren't affected by the wind. You can fish them where you want. Remember, your best dry-fly fishing is found downwind.

PRIME WATER WILL CHANGE FROM SEASON TO SEASON

shoal

shallows

WINTER

Fishing is usually slow. The fish just don't eat that much in cold water. Fish the shallow areas that are warmed by the sun.

SPRING

Fishing is usually good. Temperature is just right and fish are hungry from a long winter. You can find fish almost everywhere. Nymphs are good springtime flies.

Dry-fly hatches are starting

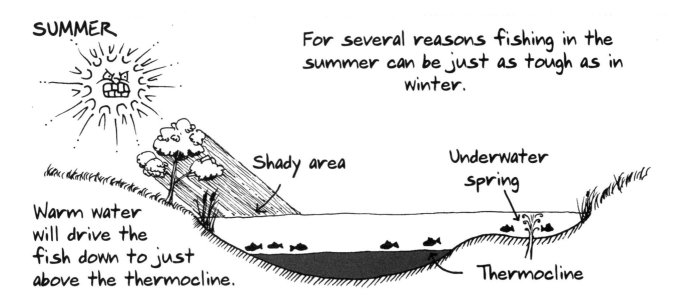

SUMMER

For several reasons fishing in the summer can be just as tough as in winter.

Shady area

Underwater spring

Warm water will drive the fish down to just above the thermocline.

Thermocline

Summer can be tough fishing, especially midday. This is a good time to fish Woolly Buggers down on the thermocline. Look for shady areas that won't warm as fast as water in direct sunlight. Many lakes are fed by underground springs so try to find and target these spots. Early in the morning and late in the evening look for fish moving into shallows to target hatches.

FALL

Like spring, fall can be a great time to fish.

Think of fall as starting when your nighttime temperatures drop into the low forties. This will start the cooling effect for your lakes. The last of the big dry-fly hatches will happen but the insects will usually be smaller than in spring and summer. With water temperatures returning to what they were in spring you should be able to find the fish holding most everywhere.

When you are retrieving, don't think of your fly as a point in space but as a sphere, whose radius can't exceed the visibility of the water.

Little
flies
have
little
spheres...

...while..

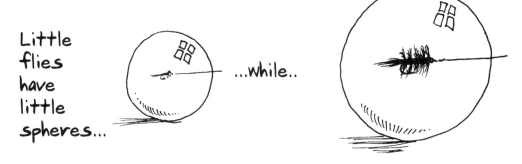

...Big flies have big spheres. Maybe the size of a beach ball. As you retrieve your fly you will be fishing a column of water as long as your cast and as wide as your fly sphere.

First, estimate the size of your fly's fishing sphere. This is not an exact science...a little guess work is in order.

third cast

second cast

first cast

Next: Count down the seconds it takes your fly to sink a foot. Do this next to your boat or float tube. Then figure out how deep you want your fly to fish and multiply it by how many seconds your fly sinks per foot. This will get you close to the right depth.

On each succeeding cast make sure you place your fly so that the fly's sphere will slightly overlap. You will find smaller flies need to have a tighter pattern than large flies. It is not a perfect system but it allows you to feel confident you covered the water.

REMEMBER THE 10 MINUTE RULE !

Like my mechanic says,
"if it ain't working ya better fix it."

The ten minute rule states: If you go ten minutes without a strike, change something. All the good fishermen have their own variation of this rule but mine goes like this. First I change my depth, then I change my retrieve, and then I change my fly. Every fly pattern gets about half an hour of exposure. On a hard day it can take up to six or eight hours to stumble on the right combination.

YOU'LL SEE LOTS OF HARD DAYS.........
BUT NOT MANY THAT ARE IMPOSSIBLE.

If a day is tough, don't give up. Often an event such as a hatch can come along and save the day. You will also see one-fish-per-fly days; every time you change flies you get just one fish, but not two. It happens every year at least once per season. On these days you will be fine if you have a lot of different patterns.

READING THE RISE

FISH CAN'T READ

There has been a lot written about how you can tell what the fish are feeding on by their rise. After thirty years of fly fishing I'm not so sure. I want you to take all that information with a grain of salt.

What I do believe is that the rise will tell you if what they are feeding on is capable of a quick escape. You will see two common rises: A gentle rise...often called a midging rise.

Here you will see the head and tail and sometimes the back.

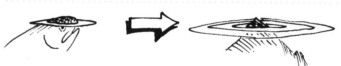

This is the rise for surface or close to the surface bugs that can't fly away. It can mean they are feeding on spinners, nymphs, Chironomid pupae or god forbid, *Daphnia*. The nice thing about this rise is that it will tell you the direction the fish is traveling.

The Splashy Rise

The splashy rise will tell you that the insect they have targeted is capable of a quick escape. It is usually associated with hatching adults. These can be midges, mayflies, or caddis flies. The nice thing about this rise is it means the fish are serious about dinner.

160

A FRESH LOOK AT ... CATCH & RELEASE

Most fishermen have heard so much about catch and release it has become like the eleventh commandment, I won't expand on its obvious virtues. One of the best benefits of catch and release is not environmental. Without proof of how small your fish really is, you can lie.

This is one of my favorites:

I JUST HOOKED FIVE FISH AND LANDED EIGHT!

GOT ONE SO BIG HE THREW UP THREE LEGAL TROUT!

Catch & release is good for fish and even better for the occasional white lie.

I CAN RELATE TO CATCH AND RELEASE

LOCAL KNOWLEDGE

There is little that compares in importance to local knowledge. This can help you on where and how to fish, and which flies to use. You are bound to meet up with all kinds of guys who will offer advice. Here is a relative rating system to gauge the quality of the information you are getting.

The first step in evaluating the information is striking up a casual conversation: Something like, "Hi! How's fishing?"

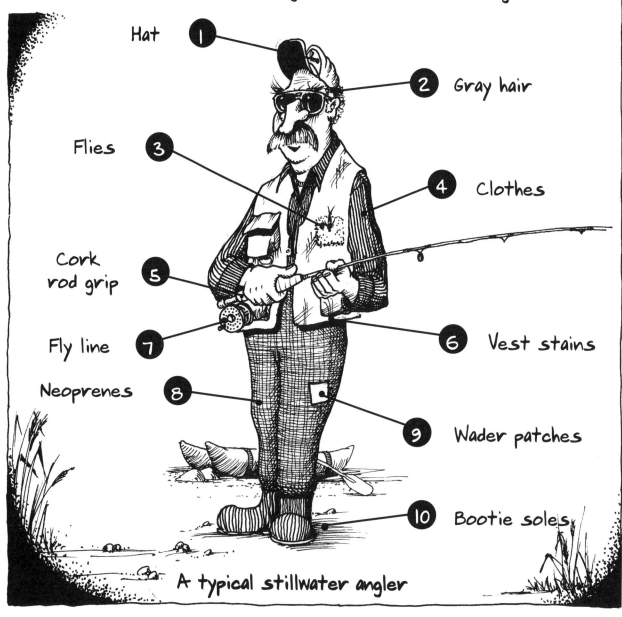

Hat — 1
2 — Gray hair
Flies — 3
4 — Clothes
Cork rod grip — 5
6 — Vest stains
Fly line — 7
Neoprenes — 8
9 — Wader patches
10 — Bootie soles

A typical stillwater angler

While your new friend is answering, check out his stuff and add points accordingly.

1 Hat: You can't judge much from a hat unless it says something like "Fred's Worm Farm." If it does, deduct 10 points, otherwise it is neutral.

2 Gray hair: Since a lot of hatches happen only once a year it can take a lot of seasons to work out all the problems. Gray hair means he is old enough to have worked out the problems. Rate him like this:

gray side burns.....+ 10
mostly gray............+ 15
all gray.......................+ 20

3 Flies: Look at his flies and ask him if he ties his own. If he says yes, add 20 points. If he says no, deduct 20 points. You can't tie flies without some knowledge of entomology.

4 Clothes: If your new acquaintance looks like he just stepped out of a fly-fishing magazine, all decked out in the latest stuff, then he has enough money to fish anywhere he wants. If your lake is not the best water in a hundred-mile radius then deduct 10 points for bad judgment. If he can afford to fish anywhere, what's he doing here? If he owns a fly shop, add 20 points. Fly shop owners gotta show off the stuff.

If his clothes are bright colored, deduct 10 points, if they are neutral grays or greens, add 10 points.

5 Rod grip: Ask him if his rod is new, if he says "no" and the handle is clean, deduct 10 points. If he says "yes" and the grip is dirty, add 10 points. It means he uses it a lot.

6 Vest stains: If you see evidence that his floatant has leaked leaving greasy stains on his fishing vest, add 10 points. If it is real grungy, add 20 points. It's a sign of heavy use.

7 Fly line: If you see a fluorescent fly line, deduct 10 points.

8 Neoprenes: Ask if he likes the brand and how old they are. Five seasons are about max for heavy use. If he says they are old and look new, deduct 10 points. If they are new but look old, add 10 points.

9 Wader patches: Add 5 points per patch.

10 Bootie soles: Drop something on the ground and while you are bent over picking it up, check out the sole on his booties. If they are worn, add 10 points.

Bonus Points: Find out where he is from. If he lives within ten miles of the lake give him a bonus of 40 points. Deduct 5 points for every fifty miles he lives from the lake.

If, at any time during the conversation you hear this...

> HECK! YEAR IN AN' YEAR OUT YA ONLY NEED ONE FLY!

then politely walk away...he is a fool. However, for those who score over 75, work them for advice. Should you get that rare guy that scores over 100, then listen to every word he has to say. Pay special attention to the patterns, size, and depth he likes to fish. Usually he will have good information on which part of the lake has springs or special bottom structure that will cause the fish to hold there in greater concentrations. Finding one of these guys is a little like finding gold at the end of the rainbow.

There is a steep learning curve for fly fishing, but you can cut years off your own curve with a couple of shortcuts.

SHORTCUTS

You can have the right equipment, the right lines, and the right flies, but if you are not fishing your water at the right time you will meet with only limited success. There are those who tell you "timing is everything." If you have twenty or thirty lakes within driving distance of your home, then it will take years to chart the proper timing for the hatches on your water, if you do it on your own. You need to have spies that give you the conditions on all your local waters. You can do this by joining a fly club. At every fly club there is generally a half hour of fishing reports...

TWO WEEKS AGO ON ECHO LAKE, I CAUGHT TEN ...

FLY CLUB

The club members stand up and tell where they fished over the last month. There will be reports that won't do you any good, like tarpon fishing in the Keys. At every meeting there are a few that will interest you. In a small notebook write down the four that are the most interesting. Now, they won't do you any good this year, but next year you will have the timing down for a trip every weekend. Most clubs charge an annual fee between $25 and $50 dollars, which is pretty cheap for the amount of information you will get.

Learning the right TIMING will take years off your learning curve!

GET A PARTNER

You can speed up the learning process by finding a fishing partner. You will go more often and you have someone to share ideas with. Since water seeks its own level you will have a hard time finding a real good fly fisherman as your teacher.

The real good fisherman will have his own partner. Look for a partner that has about the same skill level you do and discover the sport together. In a few years you will be right up there at the top of the heap.

DON'T BE A SNOB!

Don't be swayed by the guys who tell you the only fly fishing is dry-fly fishing. This is a philosophy expounded by fishermen with only average skill levels and they use it to cover up the fact. Don't turn your nose up at the spiny ray fish. Bluegills and bass are great fish for practicing your skills, like hook-setting and casting into tight places. Look for them when the trout won't play.

YOU'LL NEVER LEARN IT ALL

Often another fisherman will get it all right and start catching before you do. It happens all the time. Don't be afraid to ask him for help. Three out of four will be open with their information. As for the one who thinks fishing is akin to national security and it all should be a secret....well, he is an ass.

I still ask questions and if I can do it so can you! If it is just too hard on your ego, then look and watch his retrieve, his leader length, his fly if you can see it. Observation isn't restricted to nature.

One of the most important shortcuts...

TIE YOUR OWN

Fly tying is not only educational but a lot of fun during the off-season when you can't get out on the water. Fly tying allows you to...

* Design flies that will do what you want. You can control everything from the sink rate to the direction in which the hook rides.

* You can add your own magic. You can add a color or flash to a favorite pattern. Pick up a couple of books and take a class at your local fly shop. Once every month, during winter, pick one pattern and get the supplies to do just that pattern. In the spring, you will be well on your way to having fly boxes that handle all situations.

167

The absolute, most important thing you can do to get better is to fish! You want to fish as much and as often as you can. While you are out, use all the observational powers you can muster.

If you need a good rationale to go fishing, remember we all have a finite number of hours and someday it'll all come to an end. You might just find yourself in front of Saint Peter, if you haven't led a perfect life, then you'd better have a few good stories!!

Remember Saint Peter was a fisherman too. It might not work but it can't hurt...just don't stretch the truth too much!

Well I'm just about plumb out of things to say. What's worse, I'm out of India ink and erasers, too. Spring is coming and I'm getting a powerful urge to get out on the water. I can even hear the trout barking. I hope I have been a little help and that we meet up someday out on the water.

You've heard...

"In the end, the one with the most toys wins."

Well that ain't quite right, you see it's
really about quality and not the quantity.

"In the end,
the one who uses his toys
the most,
wins."

the Fish Bum Credo